MW00437042

Success Over Shame

Bob Harrington

"It's Fun!"

Brother Bob Harrington

Bob Harrington, C.S.W.
Chaplain of Bourbon Street
PO BOX 1445
MANSFIELD, TX 76063-1445

Success Over Shame

How to successfully defeat shame
and make your life count for good!

Brother Bob Harrington
"The Chaplain of Bourbon Street"
with Dick Newman

Foreword by Dr. Jerry Falwell

River City Press, Inc.
Life Changing Books

Success Over Shame
Copyright © 2005, Bob Harrington
"The Chaplain of Bourbon Street"
All rights reserved.

ISBN: 0-9764232-9-4

No part of this book may be reproduced in any manner
without the written permission from the publisher.
Brief quotations may be used by Pastors, Teachers,
and Reviewers for use in magazines, newspapers, or on
broadcasts when the source of materials is acknowledged.

All scripture references taken from the King James Version
(KJV) of the Holy Bible.

Graphics, Cover Design:
Jennell Bandstra • Minneapolis, MN

Editor:
Charlene Meadows • Minneapolis, MN

Publisher:
River City Press, Inc.
4301 Emerson Avenue North • Minneapolis, MN 55412
www.rivercitypress.net • publisher@rivercitypress.net
1-888-234-3559

Dedication

To Becky, my darling wife who is the essence of what the Scripture says a wife should be, "a help meet."

Knowing the shame I brought upon myself, the Church and my precious Redeemer, she loved me and believed in me as a man of God.

She practiced two of the principles of Success Over Shame, "Love and Forgiveness."

Contents

Foreword

Bob Harrington has always been one of America's greatest communicators. In his new book, Success Over Shame, Bob shares the honest truth about his personal struggles, failures and successes. No one has been more used of God to help encourage broken people to let God put the pieces of their lives back together again. Don't miss this powerful and helpful book. It will help you in your walk with God.

Shame is a powerful weapon in Satan's arsenal. When Christians struggle, stumble, and fall, Satan dumps a load of guilt and shame on us to keep us from pressing ahead for God. Sometimes guilt is necessary to bring us under conviction, break us and move us to repentance. But shame can be an ongoing self-inflicted torture that keeps us wallowing in a pool of self-pity from which we see little possibility for escape.

Once the devil can get you to believe God is finished with you, he has you right where he wants you. When you give up on God, you give up on life and that's when Satan wins. He wants to ruin your life, silence your testimony, and eliminate your influence. Don't let him get away with it! It is never too late to come back to the Lord and ask Him to turn your life around for His glory.

In over fifty years of ministry, I have discovered that God's people want to see genuine repentance followed by restoration of God's servants. They want to see that you haven't given up on God despite your own mistakes. You may not have run the race well early on, but what really matters most is how you finish. The Apostle Paul understood this when he said: "I have fought a good fight, I have finished my course, I have kept the faith."

God bless Bob Harrington, and thousands like him, who would not let Satan win the last battle. It is never God's will for us to quit. If you have fallen, get up and get back in the race. Get God's forgiveness and make a renewed commitment to make the rest of your life count for God.

Jerry Falwell
Founder and Chancellor of Liberty University
Lynchburg, Virginia

Acknowledgments

First, I want to thank my Lord Jesus Christ for saving my soul in Sweet Water, Alabama on April 15, 1958, and then three days later while giving my first public testimony, God called me to become an evangelist, a traveling preacher. But before this I thank God for my Mother and Daddy giving birth to me in the presently nonexistent community of Coxheath, Alabama, on September 2, 1927.

I want to thank God for the love of my two daughters, Rhonda and Mitzi, who never stopped loving their Daddy. A special thank you to Rhonda's husband, Chuck, for his continued encouragement. Thank you, Mitzi, for giving me four, big handsome grandsons. Much appreciation is given to the late Mayor Victor Schiro of New Orleans, Louisiana who officially proclaimed me "The Chaplain of Bourbon Street" in 1962. Much appreciation is also given to former Louisiana Governor, Edwin Edwards, for proclaiming me "Louisiana Ambassador of Good Will to America," in 1976.

Many thanks to my Lord for leading me to Becky- my loving, caring wife who invited me to come to Texas and live with her on her thirty four acre miniature horse ranch. She introduced me to her friend Dick Newman who helped me write this book "Success Over Shame."

And finally, many thanks to my friend and the best man at our wedding, Chuck Kennedy, who helped me get this book ready for you to enjoy.

Introduction

What is the one common denominator that links presidents, preachers, politicians, pimps and policemen?

Shame!

From the White House to the jail house to the whore house to the church house: shame knows no boundary. It reduces the greatest of men and women to a shadow of what they once were.

I can't speak of shame without thinking of the sorrow I've brought on my own life and my family. When you read the words "I've been there and done that!" you can be certain that Brother Bob, The Chaplain of Bourbon Street, really has been there and done that.

How can I live with myself knowing I so miserably failed the Lord who loved me and gave Himself for my sins? I have found the answer. I discovered in Christ a place where I can enjoy life again. And not only can I do it, but you too can experience success over shame.

The purpose for writing this book is not to glorify the terrible things that anyone has done. Neither you nor I should be proud of the wrongs, the sins and the despicable deeds we have done in our lifetime.

By the same token we do not perform our best as long as the storm clouds of guilt hang over our heads. You may recall a little fellow named Joe in the comic strip "Lil Abner." Joe had a confusing last name that was never pronounced the same by two people. I won't even try to write it.

Every time he appeared in the comic strip he had a cloud over him and it was raining. That's what happens when shame rules an individual's life. Wherever a person like that goes, shame rains on their parade.

Here is the good news, through Jesus Christ you can win in the fight against shame. You can enjoy the sweet taste of victory; you most certainly can have success over shame!

Chapter One

Shame Disgraces God's Grace

As soon as the prison doors slammed shut behind me I knew that was not the place for me. In a few hours however, those same doors swung open and I was free. I was a visitor with a message. I was not an inmate.

Many of the men who came to church in the Maxwell Field Federal Prison, near Montgomery, Alabama had heard of Bob Harrington, The Chaplain of Bourbon Street either over radio, television, or from being on the infamous Bourbon Street in New Orleans. They remembered the man with the red tie, red socks, red hankie, red Bible, and a red hot message that pulled no punches.

When I looked at them I could feel the pain and the guilt on their faces. Time didn't allow me to hear each man's sad tale. Time didn't allow me to learn the particulars of why they were in prison. One thing was evident—each man had a story. Each carried his own heavy weight of SHAME.

I couldn't begin to relate the bitterness they felt for being locked up or the resentment they held for the guards, the warden or the government, because I don't understand the rigors of prison life. But I do know, first hand, the terror shame brings to a man.

Bare feet and bib overalls

Today I'm known as Brother Bob, The Chaplain of Bourbon Street, but I remember the little boy dressed in bib overalls and running barefoot through the muck and mire of Sweet Water, Alabama.

(I was nine years old before I had my first pair of shoes. Now let me tell you, those shoes introduced me to stress—big time!)

Being slightly large for my age gave me the advantage of running with the bigger boys.

Early in life I learned to snitch home-rolled cigarettes. At a young age I could smoke, chew and spit with the best of them. But that first pair of shoes nearly killed me.

My poor feet longed to feel the mud and manure squeezing up between my toes. I guess those shoes were a lot like being locked up, only prison affects more than just the feet.

Life in rural Alabama was hard in those days, poverty was everywhere. Most folks like us lived primarily on the things we raised or bartered. Papa worked in the local sawmill until the depression shut it down; then he had to find a new way of making a living.

His first venture into business was a "cash-and-carry" store. "Cash-and-carry" meant you pay with cash if you have it and we'll carry you if you don't. In our case most folks had very little cash so we carried more than we took in. Needless to say that venture failed.

New shoes, new car and a radio

But Papa was resilient and before long he had another business going that did well. Good enough to buy that first pair of shoes and a new Terraplane automobile.

If you haven't heard of a Terraplane, let me tell you it was a fine machine made by the Essix Car Company. (Later it was bought out by Hudson, which merged with Nash and became American Motors eventually bought by the Chrysler Corporation.)

The Terraplane was a funny looking car especially in the front. Oh, but it was fast. Not only was the car fast, Daddy was making some important decisions and we were on the fast track to success.

Papa loaded my brother Jerry and me in the back seat of the Terraplane and drove to Demopolis and taught me my first lesson in marketing. He bought a radio; brought it back home and put it in the store. When he turned that radio on, our business almost doubled. Since we were the only ones in town with a radio, folks gathered at our store to listen, to laugh and to buy.

I used that same principle on Bourbon Street; I had a tape player with a speaker outside. I played "The Old Rugged Cross" over and over. Some of the neighboring businesses were agitated because it drove away the drug buyers and men looking for hookers, but I played it just the same.

An unending stream of the lost

Standing in the doorway of that "Chapel" on Bourbon Street I've watched drunks, drug addicts, prostitutes, pimps, thugs, bank robbers, thieves, wife beaters, child molesters, cops, lawyers, politicians, preachers, house wives and business men mingle together as if drifting on the tide of anonymity. Not all were sinners; many were good church people taking their first steps into the dark abyss of shame.

How can a man or woman who has known the marvelous grace of God be caught up in evil practices? What happens inside the heart? Are there no warning signs? Don't they feel the check of the Holy Spirit?

Yes! There are always signs to warn the child of God! The Holy Spirit tugs at the heart, but sin is deceitful.

Rarely does one fall into moral depravity on the first try; it usually starts with a "small" sin. A "little" harmless wrong, a flirtation that exhilarates, a drag off a joint, a night on the town and it isn't long until they are living it up so high, they can't live it down.

The road to the "Pit" is a downward road littered with good intentions and the wonderful grace of God cast aside by too many of His children. Like moths drawn to the flame that will singe the wings and snuff out the life, men and women run pell-mell toward the gates of destruction.

I sacrificed grace for self glory.

I took the grace of God for granted. I allowed myself to be drawn by fame and fortune and frivolously frittered away my most treasured possessions...

My FAITH!
My PEACE!
My TESTIMONY!

I became a modern day Prodigal Son!

Somehow in the glare of the bright lights of my own success I lost sight of the Cross. The music which once inspired my spirit and fed the inner man lost its appeal. I traded "Blessed Assurance" for Blues; Country Gospel for Country Western; Christianity for "Churchianity."

Amazing grace!
How sweet the sound—
That saved a wretch like me!
I once was lost....
(Amazing Grace, John Newton)
LOST

The word "lost" will echo in the corridors of hell, haunt mankind for eternity and forever bring up memories of the last rejected altar call.

LOST!

Lost that's where the devil wanted me to be. But God had something better for His wandering child, His prodigal son, His wayward preacher.

The lure of the "things" which had been so appealing to me became unpalatable, insipid, distasteful, and unappetizing.

I had tasted the heavenly gift, drank the new wine, feasted at His banquet table and nothing in the pig pen of worldly pleasure could satisfy my hunger or quench my thirst.

When the laughter of the crowd died down or my latest date had left or the booze started to wear off, I had to live with me. In those lonely hours I knew I had made the wrong decision and shame was waiting for me. Gone was the white robe of righteousness He put on me. I no longer wore the ring of authority. I was stripped of my joy, my peace, my contentment.

Then it happened!

A wonderful man of God, Rex Humbard, called me, "Brother Bob, you've been away too long; it's time to come home."

Oh, how I had longed for someone to tell me I could come back. Still ringing in my ears were the cold, hard words of my long-time pastor, whom I loved and revered, "Bob Harrington, I can't help you. You are a moral failure!"

His words were like flaming arrows which were meant not only to kill, but to burn and destroy any hope of ever returning to the love I had forsaken. I was a drowning man grasping at any straw and needing someone to throw a lifeline to me. My friend, my beloved pastor, had neither a lifeline nor a straw to help.

The regular Hell, where most sinners go, was too good for me.

His words left me with a mental picture that he thought I belonged in a special place of torment. The hell that closes in around common sinners was too good for me; I deserved a spot in the middle of the Lake of Fire.

After all, I was a traitor; I had done despite to the wonderful grace of God. I was worse than Benedict Arnold, worse than John Wilkes Booth, worse than Lee Harvey Oswald or Charlie Manson. These men had simply betrayed another man or killed mercilessly. My punishment was equal to Judas who sold his soul for thirty pieces of silver.

The preacher was right I was everything he said and a lot more. And he was right in saying he couldn't help me, because he couldn't. He was looking only at the wretch in a hog wallow of shame and depravity. He couldn't help; he didn't even try but God did!

Homecoming!

Still wearing the old tattered rags of my sin and reeking with the foul smell of the pig sty, I heard the sweet music of heaven playing "Come home."

Thanks to Rex Humbard, that certified soul winner, I caught a glimpse of the lights of home and started my journey back. According to some folks I had gone too far, stayed too long, sinned too much. They thought I could never find my way home. But I did! I'm back, stronger than ever. The glint of sin is gone from my eyes; I have peace with God.

Am I remorseful for the wrongs I did, for my transgressions, my sins against the Lord, His church, my family and the thousands of friends I let down? Oh yes! From the depths of my heart I'm sorry and penitent but I no longer carry the load of shame. I'm forgiven!

Though I was guilty of "Disgracing God's Grace," that Wonderful Grace came through for me and I am alive today because the God of heaven had a master plan that included redemption for my life. Since God plants within each of us the power of choice, He allowed me to travel a road that was far from His divine plan. I had to learn the hard way that "Father" really knows best and it is through Him alone that I can live with...

"SUCCESS OVER SHAME!"

Lord Jesus, forgive the transgressions of Your children and show them the way to live a life of total success over shame. Amen.

Chapter Two

The Bigger Shame Gets,
the Smaller God Gets.

Of all people, how could I ever turn my back on the Love that rescued me from a life worse than death and a future that had hell as its destination? Me, The Chaplain of Bourbon Street?

I had prayed with thousands to be delivered from the clutches of the devil. More than once I had prayed for the opening session of Congress. I had been commended by the president of the United States for my work among the down and outers. I could speak to one or thousands without fear. My only desire was for men and women to experience the eternal love of God.

Stoke the fire or it will go out.

It happened almost imperceptibly; the fire in my spirit began growing dim. I became more interested in what pleased me than God. I became the center of my universe. I was wrapped up in myself. I didn't realize that a man wrapped up in himself is a very small package with almost no value.

I was nine years old when my Grandmother Shoultz took me to a revival at the Methodist Church in Sweet Water and my "religious" education started. The preacher gave an altar call and Grandma encouraged me to go forward. I did—to become a member of the church; getting saved was left out of the transaction.

Salvation, not religion

What I needed that day was a good dose of salvation but that was not the way they did things. That church-joining experience set the stage for many unhappy days which would come later in life.

By the time I reached high school I realized I could make people laugh. It just came naturally to me to say things in a funny way. In the classroom when the teacher was giving a boring lesson I could always come up with a remark that would set the class off in uproarious laughter. Sometimes even the teacher would break down and laugh, but it usually resulted in my being reprimanded.

The teachers rebuke had little effect on me; I had already been rewarded by diverting the attention from the stodgy old subject with my witty remark.

When I was fourteen the Japanese attacked Pearl Harbor and World War II broke out. Papa enrolled me in Marion Military Institute High School in Marion, Alabama. He had hopes of me getting a commission in the military.

That school was nothing more than a "Reform School" where the parents pay tuition.

Stress by the lap

If I thought my first pair of shoes taught me about stress, I was in for a rude awakening. In the institution I racked up demerits like fleas on a hound. The bad part was they didn't just disappear. After so many, I learned to spell the word discipline but worse yet, I learned its true meaning.

We had one instructor who was meaner than a junk yard dog. His idea of fun was making me run the "Bull Ring." I ran so many laps I knew every inch of that place by heart. Needless to say he was not impressed with Bob the "Clown" and after several trips to the "bull ring," I wasn't nearly as funny to me as I originally thought.

Even though it disappointed Papa, by the time I graduated from Marion Military (reform) School, I wanted nothing to do with hut-two-three-four. A commission in the military was the farthest thing from my mind.

Football! Now that could really get me going.

Graduation was in itself quite an accomplishment for me but to receive scholarships from eight universities was a major achievement for a kid from Sweet Water, Alabama. I chose Auburn University and set out on a non-stop journey to the "Gates of Perdition!"

At Auburn I experienced my first chapter about life in the fast lane. It was there I drank my first beer and took up smoking for real—I only toyed with them when I was young.

BEER—smelled bad, tasted worse.

I have to tell you beer was the foulest tasting stuff I had ever put in my mouth and cigarettes made me sick, at first.

You may be one of those folks who espouse the values of these two vices but I have seen, first hand, the sorrow produced by booze.

Only eternity will reveal the tragic numbers of homes that have been broken by the bottle. I have walked the corridors of too many hospitals, prayed with heart-broken parents and preached too many funerals where alcohol was the cause.

As for smoking, one woman told me she needed cigarettes to calm her nerves. I questioned how anything that causes seven kinds of cancer, heart trouble, ulcers, high blood pressure, bad cholesterol, hypertension and respiratory disorders could be good for the nerves.

Not to mention the disruption it has caused in marriage. Can you imagine what it's like to kiss your sweetheart good morning and smell a camel?

If it took drinking beer and smoking cigarettes to be a part of the "crowd," one of the "boys," then I would belly up to the bar with the best of them.

As time went by I learned to disassociate myself from the crowd. Just because everybody is doing something doesn't make it right. It's better to be alone and right than wrong with a multitude. What America needed then and now is someone with the intestinal fortitude to go against the tide of public opinion.

Wrong is wrong!

It doesn't matter if a preacher, priest, rabbi, teacher, policeman, politician, president, pimp, judge, hooker or "desperate housewife" does it, if it's wrong, it's wrong. And that goes for more than just drinking.

Standing in the doorway of the "chapel" on Bourbon Street I knew I was not one of the "boys" any longer. I had the answer that could never be found in a bottle, a needle, a one night stand, a joint, a fix or a night on the town. I had the living Christ in my heart and I wanted to share the joy He brought to me with everyone. Through Him I could help the lost find peace with God and themselves.

They knew me by sight.

Bob Harrington, The Chaplain of Bourbon Street became one of the most recognizable men in New Orleans. I was loved by some and hated by others. Owners of seedy joints, flesh purveyors, ruthless pimps and drug peddlers hated to see me coming, they knew I was a man on a mission, I was hell-bent on releasing their victims.

It was my job as a servant of the Most High to rescue the perishing and if it meant leading a wayward woman or man out of a dive or physically confronting a pimp who didn't want to let go of one of his stable mates, so be it. I was ready for the task.

Those who lived and thrived on the flesh trade didn't like me but they respected my stand for Christ. So, how could I ever turn my back on Him and make my bed in the same type of hell holes?

I'll tell you!

Pride!

The Bible says,

> Pride goes before destruction; and a haughty spirit before a fall. *(Proverbs 16:18)*

As far back as I can remember pride was a big part of my life. I laughingly told you about my first pair of shoes and how they brought misery to my aching feet but the truth is, with all the pain there came pride. In the little town of Sweet Water all the kids went barefoot, not by choice either, they were too poor to buy shoes. When Papa bought me those shoes it told me I was just a little better than the other boys.

My pride grew steadily from that point with the new Terraplane and the radio. Those things were not even mine but you would have thought so by the way I boasted. I'm sure my parents didn't see what was happening in my young life or Daddy would have tanned my jacket for sure.

An octopus from hell!

Pride is one of those insidious evils that is hidden from even the most observant of parents. My folks didn't see it; neither did I until my life was wrecked and in a shambles. Pride was like a giant octopus rising out of an ocean of confusion, wrapping its tentacles around me and dragging me down to the netherworld of darkness below.

My heart became wrapped up in what I was doing and I believed my own publicity. I was convinced that my successes were mostly me and very little God. I was the significant one.

Bourbon Street with all its filth, craven lusts, flesh pools, opium dens, gambling halls, drug pushers and alcohol parlors had been there for years. What had God done?

Yep, it was Brother Bob Harrington that had changed the lives of the hookers, gamblers, drug addicts, pimps and other purveyors of sin.

Changed lives
are the result of the cross.

How could I be so blind as to think I could set one person free? Changed lives are the result of the cross. Jesus Christ paid the price for men and women's deliverance—not me. I couldn't deliver a cat from a light pole let alone a soul from the darkness of sin.

I was intoxicated with myself. Pride pulled a curtain around my head. Inside, the curtain was all mirrors so that everywhere I looked, I saw me. It wasn't long until I loved every mirror I saw; there wasn't one I didn't like.

The devil was certain that I received my daily dose of "Me-itis." You can be certain he laughed as I grew larger and God took the back seat in my jalopy I called life.

It wasn't by accident that the devil cunningly convinced me of my exaggerated worth. He knows the outcome of pride for he was once the most beautiful of all angels until pride was found in him and he was forever banished from the presence of God.

Remember...
Pride goes before destruction, and a haughty spirit before a fall. *(Proverbs 16:18)*

Left unchecked, pride is a one-way street to hell on earth. I was on it and had passed the last exit. What I didn't know was that crippling, debilitating shame waited for me around the next curve.

Haughtiness—pride's evil twin.

As bad as pride is, it's even worse when you realize pride has a twin named haughty. While pride specializes in destruction the end result of haughtiness is a fall. I had both of these terrible twins at work in me. I became aloof and uncaring for the very people I was sent to help.

My heart was full of pride and arrogance. I was callous, without feeling and cold-hearted. The compassion which once burned in my spirit was gone, replaced by conceit and self-exaltation. A haughty spirit was at work in my heart; my fall had begun.

Like the prodigal of Bible times, I took my inheritance said good-by to the Father, good-by to righteousness, good-by to holy living and reached for the brass ring. Since I was only going around once I wanted all the gusto I could get.

When I was told that "wine, women and song" were too much, I told them I could do without the music.

My merry-go-round's brass ring was a road spiraling downward. Down, down, down...I kept sinking lower and lower into the cesspool of sin. I longed for joy but found sadness. I looked for love but found heartache, I searched for peace but confusion filled my mind.

The master motivator

The Chaplain of Bourbon Street was no longer Brother Bob; he became Bob Harrington the master motivator.

With a new wife by my side, I set out to make a fortune and I did. Money flowed into and out of our hands like Niagara Falls. We were the toast of the motivation world. Fortune 500 Companies clambered to get us. Our seminars were sold out years in advance. We had the world moving on a downhill pull.

Rather than being happy, I kept looking over my shoulder to see if the world I had on a downhill pull was gaining on me. It was!

Time to pay the fiddler.

You and I can only run so far, so fast. Sooner or later if you dance, you have to pay the fiddler. My new marriage started crumbling! I had told so many folks that this was a romance made in heaven; I discovered thunder and lightning are also made there.

The bottle which once added spark to the lovers became more important than love. In my lifetime I had been drunk far too many times but I wasn't an alcoholic and was ill prepared to handle the daily abuse an alcoholic spouse could dish out. What started out so exciting, so appealing to the flesh, turned into a roller coaster of pain and disgust.

What could I expect? I had left the safe confines of the Father's house where health, happiness and peace were the norm and traded my haven for a hog pen.

My life was as empty as last year's bird nest!

I no longer had fellowship with righteous people, godly people or people who wanted to know about the Lord. My passion for souls was lost in the desire to make another dollar and having made it I tried in vain to enjoy the fruit of my labors.

There is no joy in the filth of a pig sty. No happiness in the heart of a son or daughter of God who cares nothing for His plan. I was losing everything I worked for and found no satisfaction in anything.

Then came shame.

Bob Harrington had never been a quitter and he wasn't going to start being one now. I thought I could back my ears like a Missouri mule and make the seminars and my marriage work but the hurry-er I went, the behind-er I got.

The answer wasn't in a bottle; I had watched too many men and women try to drown their troubles in booze only to find their troubles were Olympic swimmers. My answer, if there was one, was back where I came from. But how could I ever go back? My shame was greater than I could bear.

When I thought of returning to God my thoughts would run rampant, how could I explain to Him and to the world what had happened in my heart to make me forsake the gentle hand of the Savior and choose a life of sin and degradation?

Tormenting fear

Then the devil tried the fear factor; paralyzing fear gripped my mind like a vice.

What if Christ could no longer trust me? What if I had crossed the line, trampled His forgiving blood beneath my feet one time too many and now He would remove His hand from my life and let me go on in my rebellion until my days on earth were ended?

I wanted to pray. I needed to call on Him and tell Him how sorry I was for all my wrongs but my shame kept getting bigger and the bigger it became the smaller it made God seem to be.

Could the God of the universe find it in His heart to forgive a renegade like me? Would He? My Shame had grown so large so mountainous, so gigantic that God was nowhere to be found, until I swallowed my pride and called on Him.

One call was all it took. He was there all the time waiting for me to recognize my need and seek His help.

But what about the shame, did it all disappear in a moment of time? No! I had to learn as the ever-popular Dr. Robert Schuller says, to "Turn my scars into stars." When I welcomed the Lord back into my life He turned the tables on the devil! As God became larger, shame lost its power.

I wandered so aimless,
Life filled with sin;
I would not let my sweet Jesus in,
Then like the blind man,
God gave back his sight;
Praise the Lord I saw the light.

In the light of His presence I rediscovered life!
Through Him alone I found that I really could enjoy...

"SUCCESS OVER SHAME!"

*Precious Jesus, Lord of light and life,
come now to Your children who seek Your face. Take
away the shame and flood each life
with Your wonderful peace. Amen.*

Chapter Three

My Shame Kept Me Living on the Edge

Wow! Auburn University!

FOOTBALL!

The way I had it figured, if football didn't ring your bell, your clapper had to be broke.

At last I was out of Marion Military Institute and on my way to success and stardom via Pigskin Alley.

In the Northeast you can tell it's autumn when you feel a nip in the air and the leaves start turning, but in the south you know it's fall when the air is full of footballs. In my mind's eye I could see it all. Big man on campus, girls hanging on me like ticks on Fido, fancy cars, fine restaurants, an NFL contract that would make Papa's eyes bug out and the boys back home as jealous as a cat.

What I hadn't counted on was the other side of the line.

Let me explain!

I suited up and dashed out on the field as if to say Bob Harrington is here; the game can start. I'm still in a bit of a quandary as to whether the coach wanted to teach me a lesson or to outright kill me.

Darwin's missing link

I thought I was tough but when I looked across the line I saw the biggest, meanest, double-ugly critter I had ever laid eyes on. His front teeth were missing and instead of talking he just grunted out sounds.

He could have given credence to Darwin's Theory of evolution; he may have been the missing link.

I promise you, had he known how to write, he could have written the book on tough. As they would say in

Alabama, he was "Tuff as boot leather." Compared to him I was more like a worn out rubber-sole tennis shoe.

Somewhere in the dark recesses of my memory I can recall the quarterback calling the signal and taking the snap, that's when Ol' Ug hit me and knocked me into the twilight zone.

Football was a bell-ringer all right and he rung mine real good. All of a sudden a commission in the military looked better than ever. I called Papa and told him I wanted to join the Navy. He tried to hide the disappointment in his voice and said, "That's mighty patriotic of you, son." I wasn't trying to be patriotic. I was sure I'd be killed on the football field sooner than I would be in the Navy.

The Navy taught me more than war games.

In the Navy I started graduate studies in smoking and drinking and I enrolled in Girls 101. Young, impetuous and in an environment that has catapulted many into a life of shame and lawlessness, I learned more about immoral habits and practices than I did about war in the Navy.

A lot of folks have heard me say, as The Chaplain of Bourbon Street, I've seen every vice known to man and a few that haven't really caught on with the general public yet. I don't usually tell them I got a head start on most vices when I was a sailor in the U.S. Navy.

The war was over before I finished boot camp so they discharged me. Mom and Dad picked me up in New Orleans and got us a hotel room. They wanted to celebrate the end of the war and my coming home. Later that night I slipped out of the room and did my own celebrating. The next day, we all went back to Sweet Water.

I was lost, confused and filled with doubt. Deep inside I hated myself for what I had become.

When I look back I can see how the seeds of rebellion were planted in my life at an early age and allowed to grow.

I wanted mine, whether it was mine or not.

As a small tyke when I heard the fizz of a pop bottle being opened I would run to the room to get my "share." It wasn't that I needed it or was entitled to it, rather that I wanted it and would raise a fuss if I didn't get some.

I rebelled against the teachers, my parents, the drill master at the military institute and against everything else that didn't go my way. Later in life I rebelled against the God Who loved me and washed me clean in His precious blood.

After my "patriotic" stint in the U.S. Navy, I was able to get another football scholarship. This time I chose the University of Alabama. Maybe I thought Navy boot camp had toughened me up or perhaps Ol' Ug only played against Auburn. I don't know if my fear of getting killed was gone or if I was so lost I didn't care.

Even though I didn't understand why at the time, I enrolled in Medical School. I'm sure now it was because I felt the need to help people.

In my final year I became more interested in picture taking, not real photography mind you. In fact, I had a pretty good business going in a very short period of time. It wasn't the quality of my work that paid such high dividends, rather the uniqueness of the photos.

Generally the pictures were of classmates often in situations of compromise. I did most of my work at parties when the "models" (male and female) were too drunk to know or care.

My fee was usually paid the following day when they sobered up and rewarded me handsomely not to print the pictures or to destroy the film.

Pornography or blackmail?

I never advertised my "business." I didn't know which category it belonged in pornography or blackmail.

When I graduated from the University of Alabama I was still looking for that illusive NFL contract. But, to my chagrin, not a single offer came in. My dreams were badly shattered until I learned that Ol' Ug and a zillion of his half-cousins had made it to the big show and all they could talk about was getting one more shot at me the "pretty boy" from Auburn University.

Having been ignored by all the football scouts and rebelling against the thought of five or six more years of studying at the university level, I entered the wonderful world of selling. I figured I could sell almost anything.

Selling is where it is.

I loved selling from the start! It's always been my nature to be lovable, talk fast and slip in a humorous thought here and there. Those are ideal characteristics for anyone in sales. Especially for selling intangibles like advertising or insurance, things you can't see, feel or smell.

I took my first job selling life insurance with Liberty National Life Insurance Company. I moved my wife and children to the little town of Chickasaw near Mobile, Alabama and set out to be the number one insurance salesman in the country.

My wife and I joined every club and organization in town so our name and faces would be recognizable to everyone. My philosophy was, folks needed insurance and I was their main source to get it.

We even joined a church. It wasn't that we were believers, I just wanted to get the church go-ers to add some life insurance to their "blessed assurance" and we would all live happily ever-after.

Before long, I broke every sales record in the company. My sales absolutely soared. Success was coming my way but at the same time my marriage was going south. I spent far too many evenings in the bars, prospecting and it wasn't always for insurance business.

The next few months were pivotal in my life. I became weary with the steady diet of religious talk from my boss in Chickasaw so I decided it was time to open my own insurance brokerage in another city.

I applied with another company only to find the new boss was even more of a "fanatic" about God than the one I was leaving. The good part was I'd have an office of my own and wouldn't have to sit through those inspirational meetings any more.

My new office was in Butler, Alabama, just across the river from Sweet Water. I left my family back in Chickasaw and I stayed with my folks until I could get the business going.

In Butler I became an insurance star. I was writing policies almost faster than the ink could dry on the page. I quickly achieved the dream of every insurance man—the million dollar club. In insurance that's as exclusive as it gets.

Business was great, but my life was in shambles, my family was a hundred miles away, my wife was heartbroken and the children knew something was drastically wrong.

Success is measured in achievements, promotions and dollars.
Happiness is measured by the heart!

On the evening of April 15, 1958, disillusioned, sick and tired of television and desperate for something I didn't have, I decided to attend a revival at the local Baptist Church. That would be a good place for me to do some prospecting; it would surely be better than another bottle of whiskey or hooch as they called it down there.

God was prospecting too.

Little did I know that I wasn't the only one there prospecting. The God of the ages was also on a mission. I was there to sell life insurance; He was there to give eternal assurance. He used an able preacher from Georgia named Paul Williamson.

I tried to ignore what he was saying but every time I looked up I saw his long, bony finger pointing straight at me. At the close of the sermon the "Reverend" invited all the sinners to come to the altar and be saved.

They started singing "Just as I am," I sang with the rest but the hymnal kept getting heavier and heavier.

My mind reeled with my problems, my marriage, my drinking and my womanizing. I was as wretched a sinner as God ever let live on earth.

You can bet your boots I wasn't a goody-goody sinner who wouldn't do this or that; who wouldn't touch this and wouldn't say that. I was a rawboned out-and-out sinner. I did everything the devil wanted me to do.

Just as I am.

They started the fifth verse:

> Just as I am, and waiting not
> To rid my soul of one dark blot,
> To Thee whose blood can cleanse each spot,
> O Lamb of God, I come, I come.
> > *(Just as I am, Without One Plea,*
> > *Charlotte Elliott)*

I don't remember when my feet started moving; I do recall knocking a woman's hat off as I passed by on my way to the altar. I floated down the aisle. When I reached the front, the preacher stuck out his bony old hand. I ignored it, grabbed him around the neck and started hugging him. The pastor came over and I began hugging him, too. Tears were flowing down my cheeks like they had been dammed up for years and all of a sudden the dam broke.

> Saved by His power divine,
> Saved to new life sublime;
> Life now is sweet and my joy is complete,
> For I'm saved, saved, saved.
> *(Saved, Saved, Jack P. Scholfield)*

In my mind I kept saying, "I'm saved, I'm saved, I'm saved!"

That was the most dramatic conversion Sweet Water Baptist Church had ever witnessed. Not one soul there could have guessed the impact that conversion would make on the family of God in the U.S.

Getting saved meant making things right with God and my family. It was too bad my wife and children were not there to witness the work of the Holy Spirit on the cold, heartless sinner they knew as husband and dad.

The new creation—Bob.

I left church a new man, new from the inside out. I had to tell someone what had happened to me so I went home and told Mom.

Knowing how miserable I was and what a reprobate I had become, you would have thought she'd shout the house down. Instead her response was no response! She simply ignored me. Later on I understood why; Mom and Dad were good moral folks but they had never been saved.

They didn't know, "good morals may keep you out of jail but not out of hell!"

Early the next morning I began to realize the extent of His divine work in the heart of Bob Harrington. When I awakened I reached for my cigarettes only to discover that I had quit. I quit without even wanting to. The desire was completely gone.

Not only had the Lord taken the desire for tobacco, He had delivered me from drinking as well. At last I knew what it was to be free; free from the powers of darkness that ruled my life; free from the bonds of slavery. Free to love and serve the Master of the universe—and serve Him I did.

When He saved me, He also performed an operation on me—a "guilty conscience-ectomy." I didn't have to fill out any insurance forms or buy it, Jesus paid it all.

I had never been so happy in my life; I had never felt so good.

My next stop was in the offices near mine. The men there were not interested. Wow! I had passed from death to life. How could anyone not be interested in a miracle like that? Darkness was the problem. I had become a child of the Light and the Light was too bright for those who chose to sit in the darkness.

Bubbling joy

Joy bubbled in my soul and I could find no one with whom to share it. I went to the local druggist but before I could tell him anything he gave me a cold, hard stare and said, "I've already heard, Bob."

For the first day in my life I didn't feel like selling insurance, which was something new for me. I loved selling more than anything I had ever done.

Deep inside my heart I could almost hear a voice saying, "go tell your wife what the Lord has done for you." So I drove to Chickasaw. Joyce was skeptical, at first, but after a long talk we awakened the girls. I asked each of them to forgive me for being the rotten father and husband I had been.

Testimony time

Mentally I was fumbling with my future. Then something happened that would set it in concrete. The Sweet Water Baptist Church called and asked me to come back and give my testimony on Friday night.

"Give my what?" I asked.

"Your testimony!"

"I don't know what that is!" My problem was, I hadn't learned the language.

"Just come and tell us what happened at the revival."

When Friday night arrived I wasn't scared—I was terrified! In all my years of selling insurance I had never been afraid but that was then and this was now.

Heaven was no joke.

Under normal circumstances all I had to do was tell a joke or two to break the ice and I was off and running. But this was church and most of the jokes I knew wouldn't fit in the house of God. Besides, the Lord might be there too.

Everyone in Sweet Water knew I'd been living for the devil for thirty years. Would they believe something really had happened in my life or would they think I was a hypocrite?

What was I thinking about when the preacher asked me to give my "testimony?" I should have told him I had business in the next town on Friday night. But I didn't and I had to keep my word.

To my surprise the little church was packed and jammed. If I thought I was terrified before, that was nothing. When I saw all the people I was paralyzed with fear.

The pastor introduced me. I walked to the pulpit and opened my mouth but I couldn't get a word to come out. I turned to the organist and asked her to play "Amazing Grace." I knew that old hymn from the Methodist Church.

When we finished singing the last stanza my fears were almost gone and I began to talk. I started by telling them what a lousy husband and father I'd been. As I looked out over the audience there were several heads nodding in agreement. I didn't think they knew me that well. It proves the point that people are watching us every step of the journey. If they were taking notice before I got saved, how much more after?

A lying, cheating scoundrel

Standing in the pulpit that night I made bare my soul. If anyone questioned the kind of man I was before, they had no reason to afterward. I was a scoundrel! A lying, thieving, smoking, drinking, woman-chasing scoundrel.

But the story didn't end there. I was changed, the old Bob Harrington was dead or severely wounded and a new creation was taking his place. I told the folks in the Sweet Water Baptist Church about the old man and then I told them about the new one and finished up by giving the most blundering altar call a preacher ever gave.

It went something like this, "Ladies and gentlemen, if you want what happened to me to happen to you, just come forward. Christ will save you tonight."

There was total silence. No one moved. Not a word was said. There wasn't even a breeze stirring in the church. I thought I had blown it for sure and come Monday morning I'd be back in my office selling insurance again. But I also knew I'd be a lot happier than I had been in the past.

Then from the back of the church I noticed a woman coming forward. It was my mother. She put her hand in mine and said, "Son, I want to be saved."

Years later both she and Daddy became ordained ministers in the Methodist Church.

Mom was just the first one to come forward, after her a man who worked with my father and then my aunt Mittie. By the time the service was over, sixteen people had given their hearts to Christ.

I liked watching those people come to the Lord. A fleeting thought crossed my mind; I wonder if He is calling me to preach? I thought He was and I liked the idea.

For the next several weeks my whole life was consumed with the joy of my salvation. I breathed and talked Jesus to everyone. When I wasn't talking I was singing even though my singing left much to be desired.

A few bricks shy of a full load.

I could understand my poor wife getting tired of hearing me sing but she quickly tired of the whole "religious trip." She and my mother-in-law thought I had gone completely nuts. Not just a little wacky but totally bonkers, bats in the belfry, crazy as a loon. They talked me into seeing a psychiatrist. I led him to the Lord. To them if I wasn't drinking, smoking, chasing women and lying through my teeth, I had surely lost my marbles.

They didn't realize,
what I'd lost wasn't worth finding, and
what I'd found was too good to lose!

My time was quickly filled with speaking engagements in small churches in those tiny towns that dot the south. Some towns were so small they put both city limit signs on one post. If you hiccupped, even driving slow, you would miss the whole town.

At first I was giving my testimony, but those one night meetings became revivals before long. The first one was in Dixon Mills, Alabama. Keep in mind, I had very little knowledge of the Bible. I had never read a chapter let alone the whole Book.

I really knew the Shepherd.

Looking back I'm amazed that such a crude ministry could work, but it did. The Lord blessed and saved hundreds in those meetings. I couldn't quote the 23rd Psalm, but I sure did know the Shepherd and I wasn't ashamed to talk about Him. Crude as I may have been, there was genuineness in my heart that came through to the people. Jesus Christ took a life that was wrecked and ruined and changed it. He washed me, cleansed me and set me free.

I heard a song and thought it fit my life perfectly,

> Now when I was a sinner,
> I sinned both night and day;
> I asked the Lord to help me,
> And he showed me the way;
>
> Go tell it on the mountain,
> Over the hills and everywhere;
> Go tell it on the mountain,
> That Jesus Christ is King.
> *(Go Tell It On The Mountain)*

One of my greatest surprises came when I opened a letter from Eddie Martin, a wonderful preacher from Pennsylvania. He had heard about my conversion and my meetings. He wrote to offer me a job. "It will help you mature quickly in evangelism and satisfy your passion to win souls to Christ."

I accepted immediately and became his advance man. My job was to go from town to town contacting churches, setting schedules and taking care of all the details that are necessary for a successful crusade.

The time I spent working for Eddie proved to be of great value. I learned how to organize revivals but I wasn't getting to preach and that had become a burning desire.

Rescue missions

Before starting to work for Eddie, I had preached in several rescue missions and really loved it. I guess I had an affinity with those poor lost souls. I had been a loser to booze so I knew what they were going through.

No, I was never a vagrant or a fall-down drunk. I kept a job, drove a good car and wore nice clothes. But inside my heart I knew that if it were not for the saving grace of Jesus Christ I could have become a skid-row bum.

Many of those men answered every altar call they heard. They didn't want to be drunkards but they lacked the strength to run from the evil that was dragging them to an untimely grave.

As I preached to the "Church in Bib Overalls," (that's what the rescue missions were called), I hoped against hope that they would make a lifetime commitment to the Lord. Only God knows how many did or, for that matter, how many were dead by the next morning.

The mission field

My mission field was anywhere I could get an audience. In Mobile, Alabama it was the downtown public square.

A Christian businessman and I were in a cafeteria to have lunch. He began hitting his glass with a knife and saying, "Attention, please!"

When everyone was quiet he said, "My friend will tell you about his experience with the Lord." He then nudged me and said, "It's your turn, Bob." I stood up on a chair and began to tell them of the wonderful grace of God and closed with a brief prayer.

I didn't know that the cashier called the police as soon as I started speaking. She told them, "There's a crazy man in the restaurant ranting about God; come stop him."

Rather than stopping me or hauling me off to jail for disturbing the peace, the two policemen listened and rededicated their lives to serve the Master.

Skid-row bums, businessmen, policemen and whoever would listen heard me tell the story of Christ rescuing me from the torments of a devilish life.

My shame kept me living on the edge.

How can a man continue to live a life in absolute defiance of God? For me it was shame. Shame kept me living on the edge.

Shame kept telling me I had gone one step too far to turn back. What a fool I was, cheating on my wife, lying to my children. The only place I knew how to be honest was in selling insurance.

Hello hog-pen.

Like a hog returning to wallow in the mud, I failed everyone all by allowing sin back into my life.

Shame, bitter shame, drove me to the brink of despair and would have destroyed me but Jesus pulled me back from the edge and showed me how to live again.

This time with...

"SUCCESS OVER SHAME!"

Father in heaven,
forgive me for allowing sin to enter into my life.

Help me O Lord to seek Your face and
to walk humbly with You each day.

It is only by Your grace and love that I can live
my life free from guilt and shame. Amen.

Chapter Four

Called of God,
Tormented by Same

Knowing I needed a deeper understanding of the Word of God, I enrolled in the New Orleans Baptist Theological Seminary and took the position of associate pastor of the First Baptist Church with Dr. J. D. Grey.

I worked and studied hard to be a worthy candidate for the ministry. Dr. Grey was a wonderful mentor to me. He sensed the call of Christ on my life and did everything he could to help me prepare for the day I would walk from beneath his shadow.

He and I both knew the Lord would open a door for me where I could fulfill the drive and desire of my heart. Neither of us realized we were standing on the threshold at that very moment.

In class one day, the president of the seminary made a statement that ignited a fire inside me. He said, "Where there is a pocket of sin, there is a mission field and the closest Christian is a missionary!"

By that time, I had learned some of the Bible stories. His statement made my mind race to Simon Peter, Andrew, James and John, those raw-boned, double-fisted men of the sea, whom the Lord called from being fishermen to be "fishers of men."

If I needed my own fishing hole, and I thought I did, where could I find a better one than Bourbon Street? Anyone who has ever been there, knows it's full of "common every day suckers, sharks, big-mouthed braggarts, barracudas and good-for-nothing pikers."

The middle of hell

I opened a "salvation shop" in the heart of the French Quarter—the area Dr. Billy Graham called the "Middle of Hell."

In the ten city blocks that make up the French Quarter, you can buy anything. Men, women, boys, girls, marijuana, heroin, cocaine, dozens of different illegal drugs such as PCP, LSD and Angel Dust, pornography, homosexuality, lesbianism, sex orgies and alcohol are all on sale twenty-four hours a day. New Orleans has no closing time for its bars.

If ever a city fit the description of the one mentioned in the book of Revelation this one does. It has every sin and vice to seduce the souls of men and women. If God does not judge New Orleans, He will have to resurrect Sodom and Gomorrah and apologize for their destruction.

Since the French Quarter was to be my parish, I wanted them to see me coming. So I wore a bright red tie, matching socks, a red hankie in my lapel pocket and I carried a large red leather King James Bible.

Dressed like that it was hard to miss me, but the fire in my heart burned brighter than my red tie or socks.

I started looking for shop space but the landlords and rental agents laughed in my face. One club owner told me that he would see to it personally that no preacher ever opened an office in the French Quarter.

He didn't realize he was biting off more than he could chew. I wanted to tell him I had faced Ol' Ug on the football field and except for his foul-smelling liquor breath, he wasn't nearly as bad. But it wasn't Bob Harrington he was fighting; it was the Lord of

Glory. Dr. J. D. Grey feared for my life and asked me to back off.

I explained to him, "I have a feeling deep in my heart that this is where the Lord wants me. I'm sure this is what He wants me to do."

At that point Dr. Grey gave me some sage advice as only he could. He said, "you must be as the Scripture says, wise as a serpent and as harmless as a dove."

My wife encouraged me to go for it, she knew I used to frequent this type of place and she thought if anyone could speak their language I could. Besides, she said, if I could get just one man to straighten up and do his family right it would be worth my time and efforts.

The next day, I found a shop with a locked door and barred windows. It was near Al Hirt's club.

I once told Al that he was the second greatest trumpeter. Al looked at me quizzically and said, "Then who is number one?" I told him, "A fellow named Gabriel; he's gonna blow his golden trumpet so loud it will wake up the dead." Despite what that one club owner said about keeping any preacher from renting a place in the French Quarter, when I found the owner of the locked building, he was more than glad to rent it to me for $75 a week.

Mind you, I had a one-week lease with a renewal option. That way if anything went wrong either of us could get out of the deal.

I'm not sure if I was acting with wisdom or being like the man who wears a belt and suspenders; in case one failed the other can take over.

Whatever the case, I had my own place and I was getting ready to do hand-to-hand combat with the demons of darkness on Bourbon Street.

A cross, the Word, covered by the blood

My first official act was to hang a cross outside. It was painted bright red to match my tie and socks. I put an open Bible in the window and highlighted John 3:16 for everyone to read.

I knew if they read the words,

> For God so loved the world, that He gave His only begotten Son, that whosoever believeth in Him should not perish, but have everlasting life.

...the Word would effectuate a change in their hearts.

I moved a desk and two chairs inside and hung a sign on the door inviting folks to "Come In."

Just like Papa had done with the radio in Sweet Water years before, I set up a stereo with one speaker inside and the other outside and started playing, "The Old Rugged Cross."

I'll never forget that first day when I cranked up the sound and the music of heaven began wafting down sin's avenue—Bourbon Street.

Tens of thousands had heard Al Hirt play his rendition of "When The Saints Go Marching In." They clapped, stomped and wiggled on the dance floor but when the "The Old Rugged Cross" started playing it had a sobering effect on that hell-bound bunch.

Some of the club owners wanted me out at any cost. All they could see was diminishing returns; all I could see was saved lives.

A stripper named Sunbeam was the only visitor I had the first day, she tried to seduce me. I'm certain she was sent by one of the club owners. She tried everything in her little book but the Lord helped me counter with truth from His Book. Remember, I had my big red Bible!

Sunbeam saw me as an ordinary man, which I am, capable of sinning, certainly capable of being tempted. What she hadn't taken into consideration was, I had been washed in the Blood of the Lamb. I was clean!

She didn't know I was possessed by a passion and driven by desire. I was a willing victim of a holy vision.

My passion, my desire, the holy fire burning in my soul was to see women like her changed, liberated, set free from the chains of darkness. The love of Christ in me saw her not as a hooker, harlot, or stripper. I saw her as a lady—a saint in the making.

That first encounter brought conviction to her heart and, even though she left without calling on the Lord, I began getting phone calls that I'm sure were from her, even though no one would talk. All I would hear was club music in the background.

Two weeks passed and she came back to see me, this time nicely dressed without all the gaudy makeup. She really was a beautiful woman. The first thing out of her mouth was, "Preacher, I'm in trouble, I've got to talk to someone."

"Miss work and I'll slit your throat!"

I invited her to spend the weekend with me and my family.

She called her boss and told him she wouldn't be in on Saturday or Sunday. When she hung up the phone her face was ashen with fear. "My boss told me if I missed those two days he would slit my throat." I tried to allay her fears but deep in my heart I knew his threat was as serious as a heart attack.

I don't know how many husbands have brought a stripper home to the family. Before you try, take it from me, your wife won't like it for a minute.

I must admit Sunbeam was a model house guest; she did her best to be as straight and square as a visiting missionary.

But my teenage daughters were just a little too inquisitive to suit me. They asked questions like, "How old do you have to be to be a stripper?" and "Is your life real exciting?"

My marriage survived the weekend on the promise that I would never do that again.

It was evident that God sent Sunbeam to my office, and the weekend she spent in our home made an eternal difference in her life.

As a teenager she had taken the wrong turn. Her beauty made her the target for evil men's desires. She learned early in life that sexual favors would get her the things she wanted—things like diamonds, furs, cars, clothes and shoes. What it couldn't get her was peace with herself and certainly not peace with God.

Her weekend at the Harrington home helped her find herself and the peace her heart desired. By Monday morning, she was ready to help us change New Orleans and win the world for Christ.

Nothing is more satisfying than to witness a life completely changed. That's what happened to Sunbeam. I've never been certain where she got that name but it fit her perfectly when Jesus washed her sins away. She became a sunbeam for the Lord.

When I think of her I'm reminded of Mary Magdalene in the Bible; she was a prostitute but when she came to Jesus, He made her feel like a lady and a lady is what she became. It was marvelous to see the handiwork of Christ in the heart of the stripper from the French Quarter.

Her life, her language, her dress, her mannerisms changed completely. He erased the deep drawn lines from her face that invariably haunt a hooker. Her haughtiness was replaced with humility. She loved living because the Lord had set her free. Her life was no longer being lived in vain; it was just too short.

In a few weeks Sunbeam was found dead.

As promised, her throat was slit from ear to ear. Her boss covered his tracks well. He had an iron-clad alibi for the day and time of her murder. The ruthless killer of this beautiful woman was never found. At least, not by the police. Imagine, the perpetrator of that grisly deed was left to roam the streets of the French Quarter.

I know what killed her! It was Bourbon Street. Thank God Sunbeam made peace with the Lord before the shifty-eyed butcher found her.

Only God knows how many runaway kids have turned up dead in the dark alleys of the French Quarter beaten, raped, abused and cast aside by some sex-driven pervert.

Lives are as cheap in those ten square blocks today as they were in the most dismal days of slavery in America before the Civil War when men, women, and children had less value than cattle.

How many mothers have wept themselves to sleep night after night not knowing the tragic fate of that daughter or son who came to New Orleans seeking a thrill, only to fall prey to a flesh-selling mongrel?

How many fathers have gone to their grave in grief, waiting to hear from a wayward child who had lain murdered in one of the side streets of "Sin City," their naked body found by a pack of hungry dogs or by gawking tourists?

Demons of darkness dance with glee as the unsuspecting are engulfed by a tidal wave of lustful pleasures!

New Orleans—the French Quarter, with its annual Mardi Gras and the unending parade of filth.

No city on earth is as lewd as this one. No city on earth is more hell-bent on destruction. No place on the planet is closer to judgment.

I was a man with a message, on a mission to a crumbling world. Dying souls were crying for help and I had the answer. It was not from a self-help book or a positive thinking lecture, Christ was then, and is now, the Answer! He alone is the Source of joy each one seeks after. He alone can satisfy the cry of the heart. He alone can make life worth living.

Truth burned in my soul.

If Sunbeam's death was designed to dampen my spirit or fill me with fear, the instigator was sadly mistaken. Rather than being intimidated, I was infuriated. Righteous indignation burned within me. What had been a controlled flame became a forest fire. The fuzzy edges of my vision came into sharp focus.

I launched a campaign to win every stripper, every hooker, every drug addict, every drunk and every club owner in the French Quarter to Jesus Christ. If you have ever seen anyone pull out the stops and go full blast, that's what happened to me.

So I was flying by the seat of my pants. I didn't care; to me it was better to be flying than to have both feet stuck in the mud doing nothing! Perhaps I wasn't setting the world on fire, but I was striking every match and flicking every Bic I could find. What a pity it would have been for Sunbeam's murder to put such fear in me that I would close up shop and run to a "safe" place. Fear never entered my mind. It was as if the Lord baptized me with holy boldness. I cranked up the volume on the stereo and prayed harder than ever for those nearest hell's gates to find the chapel on Bourbon Street.

Then I put legs and feet to my prayers and began walking the lanes, alleyways and streets of the Quarter looking for the lost. Pimps hated to see me coming because when I found them abusing one of their stable queens I would step in and rescue her. Most pimps are famous for beating on women but when a real man steps in, they cower in fear.

Hands scarred by fire.

I read the story of a mother who had reached into a fire to save her child. Her daring rescue left her hands ugly and terribly scarred. Nothing was said through the years about her unsightly hands.

One day the young lady came home with an invitation for her mother to attend a special function with her at the school. "I have only one request of you, Mother," the girl said. "Please wear gloves to hide your ugly hands."

A tear welled up in the mother's eye as she looked at her beautiful child.

"Have you ever wondered why my hands are this way?" she asked.

"Yes, but we've never talked about it" the daughter replied.

"Let me tell you the story," the mother said, "When you were just an infant a fire broke out in the room where you were sleeping. Within moments your crib was engulfed in flames. They tried to hold me back but I rushed into the room, wrapped you with a towel and brought you to safety."

"I didn't realize until later how badly I had burned my hands but it really didn't matter. You were my life, you were worth more than anything to me."

Tears flowed down the young woman's face as she took her mother's disfigured hands in hers and began kissing them. "Mom, please come with me to the function, but please, don't wear gloves, I want everyone to see the most beautiful hands in the world."

When the Lord reminded me of that story I prayed, "Dear Jesus, let me enter heaven's gates with hands scarred from reaching into the flames to rescue the perishing."

Life, for me, could never be the same after the tragic death of Sunbeam. I knew what the Lord wanted to do on Bourbon Street. I had watched Him transform a stripper into a saint, a hooker into a helper and I knew if He could change her, He could do it for anyone.

I wanted to hang a big sign outside that said, "Look out devil, here I come!"

My ministry became jet propelled; it shot upward like a Roman-candle! I was on fire for the Master, reaching souls. Bringing in the lost! One here, five there, a hundred, two hundred, every place I went I talked about the Lord.

Then came compromise.

One should never underestimate the slyness of the enemy. If you look for him in a red suit with horns and a forked tail, let me tell you, you're going to be disappointed. He seldom comes that way, most of the time he disguises himself as an angel of light. Deceit is one of his most versatile weapons.

He speaks so convincingly, that if you are not on your guard at all times, he will dupe you through his chicanery.

As my popularity shot upward like a skyrocket, so did my conceit. I must admit, I enjoyed the ride to the clouds and the higher I went, the better it made me feel. There were times I felt as if I could step from star to star, skip down the milky-way and hang my hat on the moon.

One thing held me back from being launched from earth to heaven,

"My opinion of me!"

I had lassoed a rocket to outer space and I intended to stay in the saddle for a long, long time, but my rocket mount bucked me off. As quickly as I had risen to fame, I started my free fall back to earth. The climb into the stratosphere was hilarious but the fall was a torment from hell.

Words escape me to describe the terror of knowing you have miserably failed and nothing can stop the downward spiral. I plummeted faster and faster. Gone was my safety net, gone was the peace, serenity, hope and trust. I was streaking down like a thunderbolt and nothing was going to stop me.

I crash landed in the hog pen of sin.

The only guidance that existed in my free fall was the hand of my arch enemy. He pointed me in the direction of the nearest pigsty and laughed at me as I sunk in the filth of that nasty dump.

My shame made me want to drown in the black foul pit. Shame told me I could never rise again but shame had not reckoned with the resurrection power of Jesus Christ. The Ruler of the ages had a better plan for His wayward son.

Just as King Nebuchadnezzar in ancient Babylon, came to himself from his crazed condition, I came to myself. I remembered home, Father's house, the land of plenty. I was so weary of the swill of the swine parlor; I thirsted for a drink of the water of life.

It isn't the good taste of drugs and liquor that keeps the addict coming back; it's the bad taste of shame and the need to camouflage the pain.

When I reached bottom there was only one way to go—up!

Shame made me want to dig the pit deeper and stay there but the Lord stretched His nail scarred hand to me and lifted me from my place of torment.

> Once a sinner far from Jesus,
> I was perishing with cold;
> But the blessed Savior heard me when I cried,
> Then He threw His robe around me
> and He led me to His fold;
> Now I'm living on the hallelujah side.
> *(The Hallelujah Side, Johnson Oatman, Jr.)*

So much had happened, so many broken promises, so many injured lives. The trusting, the innocent, the vulnerable who had placed unconditional faith in me were still out there, disillusioned and hurting because I had backed away from the heavenly call. What could I say to them, how could I ever explain? It would be better for me to fade into anonymity. Now that the love and grace of God had touched me, washed me, forgiven me, heaven was in sight—that was enough.

You will preach again.

Except deep inside my soul, the fire of the Holy Spirit was being kindled again. The Word was coming alive in my heart and I heard Him say, "You will preach again!"

Let me share a story that fit my situation perfectly.

Hen feathers and gossiping

In a sleepy little town in Mexico there was a woman who gossiped terribly. Whatever she happened to hear, she told, of course with her own juicy little tidbits.

One day the woman was brought before a wise old judge, charged with malicious gossip.

"I understand you have some very fine hens," the judge said.

"Oh yes," she replied. She was known for having the most beautiful chickens in the town.

"Bring your finest two hens to court," the judge ordered.

Happy with his decree, the woman returned with the best she had.

"Now," said the judge, "you are to walk up and down every street in the town, plucking the feathers from these hens. **Pluck them alive!** And when you've finished come back to court."

Up one street and down the other she went plucking the feathers from her prized hens. Of course the town's folks gawked as the chickens squawked to high heaven. She kept it up until every feather was removed from those poor creatures. Then she went back to the judge.

"This is my last order for you," said the man of wisdom, "retrace your steps, find each feather and put it back where it came from."

"Impossible!" The frustrated woman shrieked. "Your honor, you know perfectly well I can never find all the feathers which are blowing in the wind and if I could, it would never be possible to put them back on the hen they came from!"

"Your statement is correct," the judge said. "It is impossible to recover the feathers and even if you could you could never put them back. So it is when you broadcast lies and falsehoods. Your words are like feathers in the wind when you spread gossip; you can never undo the damage."

Not by gossip, but in many other ways I, too, had hurt many people and injured the faith of some of His little ones. My shame tormented me until I released it all to Him. He took away the guilt, healed the pain in my soul and sent me out to finish the job I'd started.

I'm back, stronger than ever, filled with faith, hope and love, I am living proof that you can enjoy...

"SUCCESS OVER SHAME!"

*Son of God, forgive Your present day disciples
of all their sins. Wash them in Your precious blood
and help them to live with "success over shame."
In Your name I pray. Amen*

Chapter Five

Shame Turns Triumph into Tragedy

Maybe I had seen too many movies about Pretty Boy Floyd, Al Capone, Bonnie and Clyde and other gangsters. I was looking for the James Cagney type to meet me at the door; I really didn't expect what I found.

Here's the rest of the story!

In the late sixties, Life Magazine published a series of articles on the Mafia in America. It listed Joseph Bonanno, Carlos Marcello, Sam Giacana, Meyer Lansky and Raymond Petrocelli as the major crime bosses in the U.S.

Carlos Marcello, nicknamed, "The Little Man," was reported to be the boss or, "Godfather," of the crime syndicate in Texas and Louisiana. He owned the Town and Country Motel on Airline Highway near Metairie, Louisiana. He had an "office" in one of the rooms. The sign on the door of that particular room read, "Three can keep a secret, if two are dead."

After reading the articles I set out to win Carlos to Christ. I inquired about him everywhere I went. I had to find someone who knew him and would deliver the message that I wanted to talk to him. It was not easy to find a man or woman who would jeopardize their life for a preacher.

Since Carlos Marcello was a "businessman," he had to have dealings with someone. I kept probing until I found Tom Prude. Tom was a draftsman for a contractor who designed and built several buildings for Mr. Marcello. When I met Mr. Prude I told him I wanted an appointment with Carlos.

Such a request was innocent enough; at least I thought so at the time. Looking back, I can see how I was taking a risk in the natural. The good thing is that God was behind my incessant drive to meet with the regional kingpin of the Mafia. To my sheer astonishment Tom pulled it off.

Meeting the big "Little Man."

The instructions were simple, "follow me and I'll lead you to Mr. Marcello's home." Early the next morning, with my heart pounding hard, I was careful not to let Tom's car get out of sight as we sped across town to the home of an accused Mafia Godfather.

Something about that morning reminded me of the little barefoot boy in bib overalls back in Sweet Water, Alabama. He had such a simple, easy life. Now that same little boy was walking in mud and manure again.

We drove to one of the ritzy country club areas where the homes were large and beautiful with their manicured lawns and magnificent flower gardens.

Turning a corner, Tom slowed down, then lowered his window and pointed to a house. When he was certain I knew the right one, he stepped on the gas and, as quick as a hiccup, he was gone. He didn't dare stop and introduce me.

I parked my car, walked up the steps, and rang the door bell. I think I was silently praying that Mr. Marcello had been called out of town, that way I could get back in my car and forget the whole thing.

Leave the neighborhood!

The door bell played a tune I didn't recognize. I waited for what seemed to be an eternity. I was beginning to feel relieved. He must have been called away and I could simply leave the house, the neighborhood and abandon the crazy notion that God had sent to me witness to a Mafia lord.

I had a nagging thought that someone would ask how many times I rang the bell. Since he probably wasn't there anyway, what difference would it make if I rang it once or a dozen times. So I rang it again, only this time I really leaned on it.

Carlos must have been in the shower or changing clothes when I arrived because when he opened the door he was lacing his belt through the loops of his trousers.

"My name is Bob Harrington; I have an appointment with Mr. Marcello," I said.

He stuck out his hand saying, "Welcome to my home; I am Carlos Marcello."

I took his hand noting how small it was. I'm a big man and at that time I was built like an Alabama football player. The "man" not only had small hands, he was short and terribly overweight. The thought crossed my mind to grip his little hand and let him feel some real strength, but just as quickly I had a vision of the morning newspaper headlines,

"Chaplain Bob Harrington, drowns! He stole more logging chain than he could swim with."

Needless to say, I shook hands gently and briefly!

We walked down a long hallway hung with magnificent paintings into a living room with thick, soft, white carpet that gave the illusion of walking on a cloud. In the corner of the room, there was a beautiful Steinway grand piano. We sat down on a small sofa. In front of the sofa there was a simple, but elegant, marble table.

Alone—just him and me and God.

I kept looking for bodyguards to be lurking just out of sight but there were none, it was just Carlos and me and, thankfully, the Lord!

Mr. Marcello spoke softly, "I understand you want to talk to me about God."

"Yes, I want to share the plan of salvation with you." My voice was soft, too.

Most of the folks who hear me preach don't realize I can speak softly.

He was eyeing me carefully, weighing every word. It was evident that he was interested in what I had to say and why I wanted a visit with him.

"Do you believe the Lord loves you," he asked?

"If anyone does, it would have to be Him," I answered.

That could have been a loaded question, considering the predicament I had gotten myself into. After all, it wasn't every day that a preacher put out feelers to get an audience with a Mafia boss.

No time like the present to get started.

Taking a small Bible from my pocket, I turned to the verse that reads,

> For all have sinned, and come short of the glory of God. *(Romans 3:23)*

Then I asked, "Mr. Marcello, do you believe you are a sinner?"

"I know I am!" He replied.

His answer shocked me. The last thing I expected was a straight-forward admission that he was a sinner. Had he given any resistance, I was ready to quote him a mile long list of the charges the government had against him.

"The Lord wants to wash away your guilt and forgive your sins. The difference between you and me is not my goodness and your badness; rather, it's that Jesus Christ lives in my heart. He has saved my soul. He is the Lord of my life."

"Tell me more," Carlos pleaded.

I didn't realize until then that, in his adult life, this man had never heard of the love of Christ. Perhaps as a child he had heard, but that was long since forgotten. He had grown into manhood knowing only the law of the jungle, the street jungle, where it's dog-eat-dog and the top dog wins.

Only God knew how many women he had made widows, how many children he had orphaned, how many lives he had wrecked. He could give an order and men would scurry like rats on a dock to carry out his words.

Sin imprisons. Truth sets men free.

He was the embodiment of the syndicate, the head of the gang, king of the hill, leader of the pack. Yet, like a child he was asking for more truth—gospel truth, the wonderful truth that sets men free from the bondage of sin!

This was going too easily. I had hoped for a sign from heaven, but this was too good to be true. I was witnessing to a "warlord" and he was asking for more. That was my golden opportunity; I handed him my little Bible and said "You read the next verse."

The wages of sin is death.

Carlos took the Bible and in a small voice with a slight accent read the famous passage,

> For the wages of sin is death; but the gift of God is eternal life through Jesus Christ our Lord. *(Romans 6:23)*

You can't imagine what it did for my faith to see this reputed Mafia king sitting there holding a Bible, reading His promises out loud. I didn't have time to relish what I was seeing because when the fish bites, the next thing to do is reel him in.

Carlos Marcello was the biggest fish in the New Orleans pond and he wasn't just nibbling; he was swallowing the bait hook, line, and sinker!

I explained what he had just read in simple terms, "That means if you keep living in sin without Jesus, you are going to be paid off with eternal spiritual death."

"It's not just you, Mr. Marcello, it's everyone who lives in this world and dies without Christ. The penalty of sin is death. Which would you rather have, eternal death or eternal life?"

"I'd rather have eternal life," he said, in a soft voice.

"Then you must open your heart and allow Jesus Christ to come in." I took the Bible and found the next verse for him to read.

Haltingly he read;

> If you confess with your mouth, "Jesus is Lord,"
> and believe in your heart that God raised him
> from the dead, you will be saved.
>
> *(Romans 10:9 NIV)*

"I'm not sure I understand that," he said.

"I didn't either at first, but when Jesus Christ came into my heart and washed away all my ugly sins, I understood."

"It means if you want Him to become your Lord, you must accept Him in your heart and confess with your mouth that He is the living Son of God."

The mouth speaks for the heart.

"The heart and mouth work together. Out of the mouth come the things that are in a person's heart. If a man has an evil heart, he will have a dirty mouth. When a man uses cheap words he has cheap thoughts in his heart. The mouth is the broadcasting station and the dispatch office for the heart," I explained.

"Have you ever sent someone to deliver a message for you with explicit orders to say only what you said," I asked.

His eyes wrinkled and a wry smile turned the corners of his mouth upward a little. "Yes," he answered.

"That person was your mouthpiece. It's the same with your heart and mouth; you say the things that are in your heart."

"I've never heard it put that way before, it makes sense," he said.

"Carlos, do you believe Jesus died for you?" I asked.

"If it's in the Bible, I believe it!" He answered.

"Do you believe the Lord meant it when He said if you accept Him in your heart He will save you?"

"Yes."

Hook, line and sinker. Now to reel him in.

At that precise moment, my own heart was pounding with excitement. I was about to see a man humble himself before the God of heaven. A man so powerful that with the snap of his fingers he could have a person killed. He had the ability to wreck businesses, destroy homes, sink ships or cause planes to crash to the earth.

"Let's look at another verse," I said,

> For with the heart man believeth unto righteousness; and with the mouth confession is made unto salvation. *(Romans 10:10)*

"Do you believe that verse?" I asked.

"I'm trying, I really am trying," he answered.

"Do you believe the Bible is the Word of God?" I continued to probe.

I believed the Bible when I was a child.

"I have no reason not to. My family believed it; I believed it when I was young, and yes, I believe it now!"

Opening the Bible to another passage, Romans 10:13, I read aloud:

For whosoever shall call upon the name of the Lord shall be saved.

"Does that mean it's not too late for me to be saved?" He asked in a tone that let me know he wanted, and knew that he needed the peace of God in his sinful heart.

Religion separates.
Christ unites.

"Two years ago I couldn't have helped you, Mr. Marcello. I thought the gulf between a Catholic and a Baptist was too great, but I've learned that Jesus is neither a Baptist nor a Catholic and He offers salvation to all men everywhere."

I wasn't there talking to him about religion. He and I had both seen enough religiosity to gag a mule. I didn't care if he was Baptist, Methodist, Evangelical, Catholic, Lutheran, Jewish or Assembly of God. He needed Christ in his life and I was there to help him.

I was determined that neither his religious background, nor mine, would prevent him from bowing his knees in humble repentance.

Religion was the farthest thing from my mind. He was a sinner, not a Catholic; I was a witness for Christ, not a Baptist.

Carlos Marcello was ready to cross the threshold from death to life. He was only a breath away from a decision that would make an eternal difference in his soul, his heart and the remainder of his days on earth. I was praying silently that he would say yes to the voice of the Lord.

For one glorious moment, time seemed suspended. The message was complete, now he must make a choice between life and death.

Today is the day of salvation now is the acceptable time.

I couldn't wait any longer; I had to ask him the most crucial question anyone ever hears, "Mr. Marcello, are you ready, right now, to ask Jesus Christ to come into your heart?"

"Yes I am!" He exclaimed.

The Holy Spirit had done His work in the heart of a not-so-ordinary man. I had expected Carlos to be difficult and hard to deal with; I had underestimated

90

the greatness of God. While He was putting a desire in my soul to witness to him, He was preparing Carlos' heart to receive the Word.

Time and eternity merged at the foot of the cross.

"Do you know how to pray?" I asked.

His voice was even softer than before, "No."

"Let's kneel," I said, as I bowed down on my knees before the Lord, making the sofa an altar of prayer. He joined me without hesitation. I should have known that it would be no problem for him to kneel down since genuflecting is a vital part of Catholic worship.

"Give me your hand and I'll help you pray," I said reaching out to him.

Immediately, he placed his hand in mine and I led him in a prayer of repentance.

It went something like this.

Thank you Lord for loving a sinner like me! Thank you for dying on the cross that I might have everlasting life. Dear Jesus, come into my heart, forgive my sins, wash me in Your precious blood and save my soul.

I confess You as my Lord. You are alive; God raised You from the dead. Right now I put my trust in You. You are my Lord, my Savior, and my God. Thank you, Jesus, for saving my soul! Amen.

When we stood up, there were tears in Mr. Marcello's eyes.

"I'll never forget what you've done for me," he said.

Still holding the little Bible, I circled the verses we had read and gave it to him. He put it in his shirt pocket between two cigars. It looked like a little TV; the cigars were the rabbit ears.

A man without a country

As I was preparing to leave his home Carlos asked, "If you don't mind, would you come down to the courthouse at two o'clock this afternoon?"

I didn't know he was due in Federal Court that day; the government was pressing a deportation action against him.

"You don't have to be seen with me if you don't want to, but if I can just spot you in the crowd, I'd know you were praying for me and that would make me feel so much safer."

How could I refuse?

When he took the witness stand, I could see the bulge in his jacket. He was still carrying the Bible I gave him.

Another new creature in Christ

As I looked at him, I didn't see one of the nation's worst criminals, I saw a brand new creature in Christ. He began that morning as a child of darkness, trapped in the deadly web of sin, but he was washed; he was cleansed by the blood of Jesus Christ, God's Son.

During the hearing, the government prosecutor spoke, as did the defense attorney—in the end nothing was resolved. No country would open its doors to Carlos Marcello. He was, in the truest sense of the word, "A man without a country!"

On his way out of the courtroom he stopped, shook hands with me and said, "Thank you for helping me find peace with my Lord."

Dr. Grey, my superior at the church, didn't believe me when I told him about Mr. Marcello accepting the Lord.

"This is something I must see with my own eyes;" he exclaimed, "why, I have denounced him from the pulpit on more than one occasion for the wicked things he has done."

His testimony was proof enough.

A few days later the three of us had lunch in one of the fine restaurants in New Orleans. I asked Carlos to tell Dr. Grey what the Lord had done in his life. By the time lunch was over, Dr. Grey was convinced that Carlos Marcello had, indeed, met the Master and Savior, Jesus Christ.

Carlos and I became good friends and not coincidentally, after that, a lot of the doors in the French Quarter that had been closed to me, miraculously opened up. And he began to support my ministry.

I never questioned him as to why he didn't leave the mob. It is one of those mysteries the Lord will explain to us when we get to heaven. It was evident that the mob activity in New Orleans changed significantly after his conversion. It was more humane, softer than it had been before.

The day Carlos Marcello died, I felt as if I'd lost a close family member.

From that fateful day when I rang his doorbell and wanted to run and hide before he opened it, until I received the news of his death, I knew him as a friend. Not as a gangster, an outlaw or a Mafia mob figure, but as a loving Christian friend and supporter of the Gospel.

I've laughed many times when I've relived those quavering moments when I stood outside his house not knowing what might happen to me for meddling in the life of a notorious mob-boss.

As the word spread throughout the French Quarter that there was a haven for the lost; a place for the weary to find rest and refuge, the little "Chapel" on Bourbon Street became busier and busier for Christ.

Women of every description, white, black, brown, red and yellow came seeking help. Not just strippers and hookers, there were waitresses, housewives, secretaries and hotel workers. Everyone had a story to tell and each one needed someone with whom to share their burden.

How many came to the Chapel for help, a hundred, five hundred, a thousand, before the seeds of self-importance began to sprout? I can't answer, all I know is that one day I saw myself as the answer to each woman's need. It was me with a capital "M".

Such erroneous thinking spelled doom to the wonderful soul saving ministry God had entrusted to me. I sadly admit the "M" on me was more important than the "J" on Jesus.

When that happened, God had to let the little boy in bib overalls walk through the mud and manure one more time! That's because God hates self-importance!

I had no answers for my shame.

It was not until after Carlos' death that I began my slide back into sin and depravity. Thank God, he was never affected by the adverse reports of my life. My shame would have been ten times worse had I been forced to face him with answers I couldn't give.

Shame turned a series of triumphs into an almost endless string of tragedies. Heartache and failure dogged my footsteps. Everywhere I turned I saw what I could have been rather than what I had become.

While the world laughed and drank its Scotch on the rocks, shame mixed a bitter cup of marriage and business for me and called it "Life on the Rocks."

Broke, humiliated and haunted by unfulfilled dreams, I finally quit running from the Answer.

> My soul in sad exile was out on life's sea,
> So burdened with sin and distressed,
> Till I heard a sweet voice saying,
> "Make **Me** your choice;"
> Then I entered the "Haven of Rest"!
>
> I've anchored my soul in the "Haven of Rest,"
> I'll sail the wide seas no more;
> The tempest may sweep over the wild, stormy deep,
> In Jesus I'm safe evermore.
> *(The Haven of Rest, Henry L. Gilmour)*

In my darkest night, Jesus welcomed me back. Strangely, He made no mention of where I had been or what I had done. He simply brought me to Father's house and clothed me once again with His robes of righteousness.

Shame turned triumph into tragedy. Jesus turned tragedy into triumph and gave me...

"SUCCESS OVER SHAME!"

Eternal Savior, Lord of all creation,
have mercy on your wayward children,
draw them to Your precious, bleeding side.
Work Your work of righteousness in our lives
that we may show the way of life to others. Amen

Chapter Six

My Dreams Were Shattered by Shame

It's better to set your goals high and just get half than to set them at nothing and get the whole thing.

I have dreamed big dreams all my life.

Even as a child I hated poverty and wanted more out of life than a hand-to-mouth existence. I never understood why the boys I ran with in school were content with status quo. They never fancied themselves as anything but dirt poor farmers. Most were from destitute families; poverty was a way of life for them.

Many were destined to be sharecroppers just like the past four or five generations before them.

It never occurred to them that they could do better or have more than their mammy and pappy. They acted poor, lived poor and were poor because they thought poor.

Contrary to many people's opinion, being poor doesn't make a person good or bad. I've known some godly folks who were as poor as church mice. By the same token, some of the meanest, orneriest critters who ever drew a breath were too poor to rub two nickels together.

I've known some very rich folks who were as humble as a piece of corn bread and some who were dirt poor and as proud as a peacock.

Money, in and of itself,
is not the answer.

I read an interesting story about a woman who died of malnutrition in the western Oklahoma town of Cheyenne, back in the fifties. She lived by herself in a small house that was little more than a shack.

It was not unusual to see her going about town with a bag full of things she had rescued from people's trash cans. Everyone thought of her as being the poorest of the poor.

When she died, the coroner listed the cause of death as starvation. Yet, when they started to tear down the shack where she lived, they found over one hundred thousand dollars in cash hidden in the mattress, between the walls and under the floor. In today's economy, that's equal to about a million dollars.

She no doubt remembered the stock market crash in the twenties and didn't trust the bank with her cash. It's hard to imagine, she died for want of food even though she had enough money to feed the entire town for a long, long time and to live in one of the nicest houses around. But she starved to death.

Being broke is a condition. Being poor is a state of mind.

Her money bought her neither food nor clothing nor decent shelter. At night, when she laid her weary body to rest she, no doubt, heard the rustling of the money in her mattress but it did her no good. She was poor, but her poverty was a state of mind.

I remember the hard times of the twenties and thirties. Back then almost everyone struggled to make ends meet. I still recall the day Papa came home and told Mama the saw mill was shutting down. They didn't know how they were going to feed and clothe two perpetually hungry little boys but they did not give in to despair. Rather than give up, Papa became an entrepreneur.

He opened his first store and everyone's poverty helped him go broke, but that didn't quench the fire in his spirit. He simply went to another town and started again.

Mama and Papa worked hard and pulled together to make the store a success. When Mama wasn't helping with the store, she was in the kitchen cooking or canning. She must have known that the way to a man's heart is through his stomach because she kept Papa well fed and he never strayed from his love and devotion to her. My, my! How that woman could cook!

Forever etched in my memory is the smell of homemade bread baking in the wood stove. And in the summer, when peaches were plentiful, and cheap, the aroma of fresh peach cobbler wafting through the little house and out into the yard, where my brother and I were playing, was enough to make us think we were starving to death.

There were times when we were temporarily broke, but the Harringtons refused to be poor.

As a result, sharecropping and being penniless were never appealing to me. Even as a child I knew instinctively that there were places to go, sights to see and fortunes to be made in this great, big, wonderful land called America.

Shoot
for the moon!

An elderly black Mama used to say, "Honey, shoot for the moon and if you land among the stars you're still walking in tall country!"

Her astronomy may not have been correct but her message was fantastic.

I had high and lofty dreams of playing professional football when I attended the University of Alabama, but when it was evident the NFL scouts failed to appreciate my talents or see my potential as an outstanding player, I moved on to the next level of life.

My goal—be #1!

With football behind me, I embarked on a journey to be the best life insurance salesman in the state of Alabama, but that was just an interim goal. I really wanted to be the top dog on the national scene.

It didn't take long for me to climb the ladder of success because I was dedicated to my goal.

You may recall the golfer who was called "lucky" by another pro on the tour. He answered, "Yes, and the harder I work, the luckier I get."

My success in selling, like his in golf, was in no way equated with luck. It was the result of hard work and determination.

Luck was what folks needed at the gambling table, I had a goal!

Majoring in mediocrity was never my cup of tea. So when the Lord sent me to Bourbon Street I went there with the idea of plowing under every hell hole, liberating every hooker, delivering every drug addict and saving every hell-bound sinner from the clutches of sin. I was dreaming big when I opened the doors of that boarded up office and started playing Gospel music over the stereo in the heart of Satanville.

I was dreaming big when I told Sunbeam there was hope for her troubled soul and when I set out to win Carlos Marcello the head man of the Mafia in New Orleans.

My dreams were big when I envisioned a safe harbor for the abused women of the French Quarter, and for the lost who roamed the streets looking for one more fix from a needle or one more swig from the bottle.

The bigger I dreamed, the more God did. It was as if He was saying "Son, if you can dream it, I can do it!" I lived with the philosophy, if you're going to rip your pants you might as well rip them big for God.

Success was like bananas, it came in bunches.

Whatever I put my hand to, worked for the Kingdom of heaven. It wasn't long until pastors in other cities were inviting me to fill their pulpits and to help them inspire their parishioners to become soul winners. I was trying to start an epidemic of soul-winning across the land. Success came in bunches.

Somewhere along the way I had been exposed to the fervor of the old time Nazarene preacher, Uncle Buddy Robinson.

He was noted for praying: "Lord, give me a backbone like a saw-log, and a determination like a bull dog; help me chew on the devil as long as I have teeth, and when they're gone, help me gum him 'til the day I die!"

Satan's Saint—Madalyn Murray O'Hare.

As church doors opened to me across the land, so did radio and TV. It wasn't long until I was going toe to toe and nose to nose with hell's heroes on live radio and TV talk shows.

Madalyn Murray O'Hare was at the pinnacle of her success. In 1963 she almost single-handedly destroyed the centuries old American tradition of prayer in the public schools.

While the average church member was singing,

In the sweet (give me some meat)
By and by (give me some pie)
We shall meet on that beautiful shore,
(give me some more)

Madalyn was making history with her Supreme Court ruling to outlaw prayer and Bible reading in the schools. It is a decision that has plagued our nation ever since.

I sat opposite Mrs. O'Hare waiting for the TV camera to turn to us. We were the stars of the day. It was billed as the debate of the century, me talking for Christ and her denying there was a God.

Madalyn, the avowed atheist, bright, intelligent, witty and very personable and Bob Harrington, a country boy preacher from Sweet Water, Alabama, going head to head about God.

She later told me it was hard to make theory believable in the face of experience. She had debated doctors of theology many times before and in many cases made them look like bumpkins. The difference was, those men were speaking from book knowledge; I debated the reality of salvation from the position of regeneration.

The fire of hell burned in her eyes.

Madalyn Murray O'Hare could have been the kindly grandmother of storybook fame except she had the look of hell in her eyes.

Beneath the demure, proper and sometimes almost reticent exterior lay a coiled cobra ready to strike. Make no mistake, she was as full of the devil as a human could get. She had neither morals nor principle.

When she became an associate of Larry Flint, publisher of the infamous Hustler magazine, she made it public that she was in favor of prostitution, bestiality and pornography. She was quoted as saying, "Whoever does not like pornography should not purchase it, read it or lick its pages."

My heart went out to Madalyn O'Hare. She was lost, hell-bound, and without hope. I've never understood why she had such anger against God. What had happened in her life, as a child or as a teenager, to enrage her to the point that she would sell her soul to the prince of darkness?

We debated in thirty-seven cities and eighteen times on the Phil Donahue show. Each time we met I told her that I was praying for her. I continued to pray for her—that her heart would be changed before she was swept into eternity. I can only hope that somewhere along the way she had a change of heart.

Eternity never ends.

The last stanza of the wonderful old hymn "Amazing Grace" has a haunting message, it says:

> When we've been there ten thousand years,
> Bright shining as the sun,
> We've no less days to sing God's praise
> Than when we first begun.
> *(Amazing Grace, John Newton)*

Think about it, ten thousand years into eternity and we've only just begun. The sobering truth is, those who enter the region of the damned face the same eternity. When they've been in hell ten thousand years, they have no less days, than when they first begun. Eternity is never half over.

No man ever born loved what he was doing more than I loved sharing the Gospel, whether it was to one lost soul on Bourbon Street, or to thousands in churches or to millions via radio or television. I would have witnessed to the devil himself if I could have gotten him cornered.

I adopted this motto for my life,

> I will not ponder at the pool of passivity,
> Nor meander down the path of mediocrity;

I will fight for what is right,
And I will win the souls of men.

My dreams
turned to nightmares.

The change was so subtle it was unobserved—especially by me. At first, it was just little things. Appointments cut into my prayer time. I had to catch a plane so there was no time to read the Bible. A word spoken sharply to an associate, to my wife or one of my daughters—surely they understood that I was under a great deal of pressure. I always meant to apologize but again the timing was never just right.

At first, there was nothing major to run up the warning flag that I was going astray; rather it was little inconsequential things that tarnished my halo and hurt the faith of others.

The devil made me do it.

You may recall a TV show that was popular several years ago starring Flip Wilson. One of his weekly scenes was him dressed up like a woman called Geraldine, her famous line was, "The devil made me do it!" Anything she did wrong was never her fault. I've known a lot of Geraldines in my lifetime and every one of them have blamed their failures on the devil.

I don't blame anyone but myself for the sins I committed. The devil simply laid it out before me and like a big mouth bass I took the bait. I have accepted the full responsibility for my failures.

A prominent minister in the Dallas, Fort Worth Metroplex teaches his associates that they can never allow themselves the "luxury" of a second look.

"When speaking to a woman," he tells his troops, "always look at her from the neck up; don't let your eyes wander, for the eye is the gateway to the soul." In that man's personal life he has maintained the decorum of a man of God. There's never been a moral scandal linked to him.

I allowed myself that tragic "luxury." At first it was an innocent glance at a plunging neckline, then a short skirt. From there the story was as predictable as the first man and woman's sin. The devil didn't force Eve to eat; he just got her to look at the forbidden fruit.

I sinned of my own free will.

It would be a cop-out for me to say the devil made me do anything. I was a full-grown man. I sinned of my own volition. I should have known, I should have been more aware of my surroundings. Most of all, I should have seen the change that was taking place in my heart and actions.

Just as success came in bunches so did failures!

My drifting took me far from the security of my calling. Once I was possessed by a passion for souls, but sin replaced that with a passion for money. Once I was driven by a desire to change lives for Christ. That drive was changed to lust—filthy, hellish lust. I was no longer a conqueror with a holy vision; I was the butt of the devil's worst joke.

I tried hard to keep my equilibrium. Tell more jokes, keep folks laughing. More seminars! If I could just do more seminars!

Nothing worked because my soul was out of sync with the Lord. I told jokes and people laughed but my insides were aching. I did more and more seminars telling corporate America how to be successful, how to

114

climb to the top. But with each seminar I sank deeper into the eternal abyss of sin and shame.

"O wretched man that I am!"

Several hundred years ago a man named Paul penned the words to sum up what my life had become, empty, void, without purpose and without meaning. Paul's words fit me perfectly, "O wretched man that I am!" *(Romans 7:24)*

Something within cried out, "Will the real Bob Harrington please stand up?" To my chagrin there was no stand up left in Bob Harrington. I was defeated; shame had shattered my dreams. All that was left of me was the pitiful shell of what used to be. If eyes mirror the soul, then it should have been easy for the most casual observer to see the emptiness in my hollow sockets.

Gone was the spontaneous laughter that had characterized my life since childhood. Gone were the lofty dreams of winning lost souls. Gone were the dreams of a safe haven for hookers from their pimp masters. Everything I held dear was gone. Hope— gone! Family—gone! Ministry—gone!

The reason I struggled with life is that I carried a dead spirit, a dead mind and a dead body. I was so dead the undertaker was past due at my house.

I was a failure as a father, husband and minister—a spiritual and moral failure. It's no wonder that life had lost all meaning. I ceased to live; I simply existed from one miserable day to the next.

When the sizzle fizzles

In my haste to desert the ministry, I made no provision for life when the sizzle fizzled. Being a reasonably intelligent person, I should have known that the pleasures of sin last only for a season. Rather than counting the cost, I plunged in head-first only to find the pool I had chosen for my midnight swim was a cesspool of sin and degradation.

When the bubble burst, I had no place to turn. Burning bridges had become a commonplace thing for me. If anyone didn't like what I was doing, I had no problem whatsoever telling them they could take a one way trip to hell.

I dreaded the thought of living, but I was in no condition to die.

I must have been a pathetic sight going through the motions of a normal person. I ate without tasting my food, drank water that never quenched my thirst, slept on a bed that felt as if it was filled with thorns and briars. The bags under my eyes made me look like I was a first cousin to a basset hound.

When would the charade end? How long could I continue to be the devil's puppet and dance when he pulled the strings? I thought I could stop whenever I chose, but once I linked up with the forces of darkness it was not easy to jump ship.

I learned the hard way,

The devil will take you farther
than you want to go.
Keep you longer than you want to stay.
And charge you more than you want to pay!

If ignorance were bliss, I'd have been a blister.

Like thousands of others I was deceived. I thought the music would never stop, the thrill would never end, the pleasures would live on forever. At a ripe old age, I'd shuffle off this mortal coil in a state of eternal bliss. I told my friends I was so happy if I were to die it would take the mortician three days to get the smile off my face.

But the orchestra hit a sour note. My roller coaster jumped track and what I thought was pleasure, turned to ashes. My dreams were dashed to pieces on the rocky shore of sin. I had nothing to which I could anchor my lifeboat. I was a man out of fellowship with his God.

As the stomach turns

The TV networks could have made a daytime soap of my life and named it "As the Stomach Turns." Sad, tortured and disillusioned by the mistakes I had made with my life, I could easily have followed the footsteps of the original Judas had it not been for the tugging at my heart by our loving heavenly Father.

In the darkest hour of my existence, I had at last come to the end of my rope. I was tormented with shame, nothing was meaningful. Surely, my time was running out. Sin had driven a wedge between God and me. I felt like an island totally isolated from His divine presence. It had been years since I had prayed, really prayed, something I sorely needed to do.

That's when God's obedient servant, Rex Humbard, a full gospel preacher, made the phone call that changed my life. He could have ignored the Holy Spirit's voice. Who was I that he should waste a precious minute dealing with me? Others had written me off. Rex could have done the same, but he didn't. He befriended me and invited me back into the family of God.

To my sheer astonishment, the Lord was waiting for me when I turned to Him. He knew every vile sin I had committed every blasphemous word I'd spoken, every lewd thought that had coursed through my mind. Yet He was there with arms wide open to welcome me back.

The God of the second chance.

The goodness and the marvelous grace of our God is overwhelming. He really is the God of the second chance.

He should have cast me aside like a filthy garment and turned His attention to someone more worthy of His love. I had trampled His goodness and grace beneath my feet in my haste to live my own life the way I chose.

But He didn't.

Jesus, the Son of God came looking for me through the voice of Rex Humbard.

The words of that great old Baptist hymn fit the occasion:

> Take my will, and make it Thine;
> It shall be no longer mine.
> Take my heart, it is Thine own;
> It shall be Thy royal throne.
> Take my love, my Lord,
> I pour at Thy feet its treasure store.
> Take myself, and I will be ever, only, all for
> Thee.
>
> *(Take My Life and Let It Be,*
> *Frances R. Havergal)*

Surrounded by His love, bound up in His everlasting grace, I poured out my heart in repentance to Him and He accepted me back. Not only did He bring me back but He lit the fire in my spirit again and sent me out to complete the job He called me to do.

Last of all, He removed the shame, the crippling, debilitating shame that plagued my heart and filled me with despair. He gave me peace. Peace with Him and with myself. With that peace He renewed the vision to reach the lost and sent me out to love those who have left, back right.

My dreams were shattered by shame. But He is the a Master who picks up the broken pieces and puts them together again.

I am living proof that through the grace and love of Jesus Christ anyone, anywhere on the face of the earth, regardless of what they have done, can enjoy freedom from sin.

Despite what the devil says, and no matter what folks may think, when a man or woman turns with a whole heart to God, He will deliver them and help them live with...

"SUCCESS OVER SHAME!"

*Precious Savior, stretch forth Your hand
to the wounded, heal their troubled spirit
and give them peace,
for You are the Prince of Peace. Amen*

Chapter Seven

From the Mountain of Glory to the Valley of Shame

San Antonio is known the world over for the Alamo, where a rag-tag band of brave men withstood General San Jacinto and his Mexican army. And it has the famous river walk on the banks of the San Antonio River which flows through the middle of downtown. It is a favorite spot with thousands of tourists each year.

Back in the 60's, there was one place more popular than the Alamo. It was the Green Gate Club located on the river walk and St. Mary's Street.

Here's the story of
the Green Gate Club!

The owners of the club, Evelyn and Guy Linton were two of the most likable people God ever let live. They enjoyed the same things and were a dynamic team for creative ideas.

When it came to making money, they had few peers, even though their backgrounds were as different as night and day.

Evelyn was born in San Antonio; she was the last of nine children. Her mother was Catholic and her father, Baptist. She grew up in a close-knit family. Unfortunately only five of the children survived to be adults.

At age six, Evelyn was baptized and was educated in the convent most of her school years. For the most part, she lived a religious life. Keep in mind that's all it was, religious. At no point did she have an experience with Christ during her childhood.

I don't say that to cast a reflection on her upbringing. Children have come from every church group, Baptist, Methodist, Lutheran, Pentecostal and others—without having a change of heart.

Like so many families in America, she and her sister went to Mass on Sunday alone. Their parents didn't attend church.

Dance halls, bars, liquor stores

Evelyn didn't see a lot of her dad. He was always busy making a living running bars, dance halls and liquor stores. On those rare occasions when her dad took her with him, she slept in the car until the joint closed. She never liked going into the bars; she hated the smell of beer.

As a little girl and on into high school and college, Evelyn dreamed of some day becoming rich and famous. She didn't know how rich or famous she was to become or what would bring riches and fame.

Not long after she enrolled in Our Lady of the Lake University, World War II broke out so she got a job at Kelly Field. She thought by working at the base she was being patriotic and fulfilling her duty to the nation.

Sheer determination.
Rare intelligence.

Evelyn was never one to sit around and wait for something good to come along. Rather, by sheer determination or rare intelligence, she made things happen. By the time she was twenty years old she opened a jewelry business in the old downtown section of San Antonio.

Not many women at the young age of twenty have enough wisdom to jump-start an import business and turn it into a profitable enterprise the way she did. Jewelry was hard to find during the war years. When she found out she could import silver from Mexico, she was off and running.

To be a successful merchant an individual has to be "street smart." Evelyn Linton certainly was that. She heard about a man in the Majestic Building who bought and sold jewelry. This was her "golden" oops, "silver" opportunity.

Realizing this could be her first big sale, she packed some of the finest pieces and went to his office. But in her excitement, she dropped everything on the floor.

Being a gentleman, Guy helped her recover all the jewelry and thus a romance was born. Before she left he asked her to go with him to a football game. Not being a sports nut, Evelyn declined. Guy, not accustomed to being turned down, promptly suggested a matinee movie at the Majestic Theater, which by "sheer coincidence" was located in the same building.

During the movie, Guy held her hand and at that moment Evelyn knew Guy Linton was the man of her dreams even though he was thirteen years older and had a son from a previous marriage.

They dated four months, then tied the knot before a Justice of the Peace in 1945. Their whirlwind romance never stopped until the day Guy went home to be with his precious Lord.

Many times Guy remarked that the five dollars he gave the Justice of the Peace to perform the ceremony was the best investment he ever made.

Business vs. honeymoon

After the ceremony came the decision, business vs. honeymoon. It wasn't difficult for either of them. They were so focused on their businesses and making money, they opted to postpone the usual "honeymoon" until they had the funds to really do it big.

Two people could not have come from more diverse backgrounds. She was from a Texas family which had plenty of money; Guy's background was one rife with the rigors of pain and heartache. His father died when Guy was only five years old, so he grew up working hard from dusk 'til dawn on a farm in Tennessee. He picked cotton and did anything else that needed to be done to help his mother. Like Evelyn he dreamed of some day being rich and famous.

Dreaming but not daydreaming.

To really dream is to have a goal and a plan to achieve it. To daydream is to sit around wishing it would happen. Neither Guy nor Evelyn were daydreamers. They wanted to be rich and famous and they knew the first step in that direction was to formulate a plan. Then work with all their might to make it happen.

It isn't just working hard, but working smart and diligent, doing your best always.

I heard the story of an old carpenter who was a master at his trade. For many years he worked unflaggingly for a contractor. He built some of the finest homes in the town gaining a favorable reputation both for himself and the now successful contractor.

One day as he finished one of the most beautiful homes he had ever built, he told the contractor it was his last. He wanted to retire and even though he needed the money, he was tired and wanted to spend more time with his wife and extended family.

The contractor gently persuaded him to do just one more house for him, promising that it would be the last. The old carpenter reluctantly agreed. But as he built, he cut corners and was not as meticulous as he was noted for being. It was obvious that his heart really was no longer in building beautiful homes.

Finally, when the last nail was driven and the painter did his touch ups the carpenter gave the keys to the contractor. But he was unhappy with himself; he had not done his very best.

The contractor promptly handed the keys back to him and said, "The house is yours, it's my way of saying thanks for all the years of faithful service."

How sad that he had not gone the extra mile, done the job in the manner he knew, and built something he could have been proud to show his friends.

Evelyn and Guy were not like the old carpenter. They were focused on the goal of being rich and famous. They planned and built as if their lives depended on it.

One night while on business in Dallas, they went to see a floor show in a night club. The star of the show was the world-famous stripper, Candy Barr. They were impressed that people lined the streets waiting to get into the club.

After the show Evelyn said, "Guy, why don't we go back to San Antonio and put in a club like this? If we can find a place overlooking the San Antonio River, think of the business we can generate. We'll make a fortune."

The Green Gate Club

The decision to open a burlesque show was nothing less than a stroke of genius. Their bevy of beautiful young women brought in hot-blooded Latinos by the bus loads. But it wasn't just the Latinos who packed the place. There were military bases all around San Antonio.

Soldiers didn't make a lot of money, but they enjoyed spending what they had and the Lintons didn't mind sending them back to the base happy and broke. Their club was the hottest spot in San Antonio even more popular than the Alamo for many years.

Guy and Evelyn staged up to six shows a night. The Green Gate Club was the largest and became the "most famous strip club in Texas." Evelyn was known as "The Queen of Burlesque" and Guy was called "The King of the Strippers."

Dallas had its Candy Barr, but they had a whole bag of sweet treats.

Little did Evelyn realize when she suggested that they open the joint that it was their ticket to fame and fortune beyond their wildest imagination.

The Lintons bought a mansion, a ranch home with hundreds of acres, a lake home and had a twenty-four hour maid service. They had so much money they could have had hot and cold running towels. All of it was made possible by Evelyn's knack for training pretty women to dance in a seductive way.

Like a spider spinning its web to trap an unsuspecting fly, Evelyn lured young ladies in. Once they were caught in the web of demonic deception it became their turn to "catch" the lustful clowns who frequented the shows.

Guy was especially good to Evelyn, never denying her anything she wanted. He gave her diamonds, furs, fancy cars, and expensive clothes.

The jewelry he designed for her made the Mexican silver pieces she brought to him the day they met, look like something you find in a Cracker Jack box.

While the press dubbed her "The Queen of Burlesque" to Guy she was, in real life, his "Queen."

The Green Gate was open for seventeen years and was known throughout the world for its beautiful girls. On several occasions, managers of Las Vegas shows and casinos came trying to "persuade" the pretty country girls to "make it big" in Vegas.

A preacher from New Orleans

Evelyn and Guy's lives were drastically changed one night when, of all people, a preacher from New Orleans walked into the Green Gate Club and asked if he could preach there that night.

I was in San Antonio for a crusade and as I often did, I was on the prowl for a pocket of sin. I was never satisfied to just win those who came to church.

I wanted to bankrupt the devil and empty every hell hole in town.

When I told Guy I'd like to preach in the club he gave me that "what kind of weirdo is this" look, and excused himself to go find Evelyn. He later confided in me that he thought I was drunk or crazy as a loon.

Evelyn, on the other hand, saw it as an opportunity to get publicity and bring in more customers.

She introduced herself and asked, "Mr. Harrington, why do you want to preach in our club?"

Jesus preached at the local watering holes.

"I've studied the life of Jesus for several years," I told her, "and I'm convinced that if He was here He would want to preach at your club. When He was on earth He didn't spend all His time in church, He preached at the local watering holes. He always went to the places where people were hurting."

"Will you make them feel guilty?" She asked.

"No" I answered, "they already feel that way. Jesus came to take away the guilt and set them free."

So I preached there that night. I gave the club and the crusade some publicity but other than that, as far as I could tell, it was an uneventful service. I didn't realize the seed was sown in Evelyn's heart; seed that didn't die when I left San Antonio.

Easter sunrise in a downtown mall.

Two years later, I was invited back to San Antonio to preach the Easter Sunrise Message at the downtown mall. I was unaware that Evelyn was in the audience that morning. She wore dark sunglasses and a big hat to help disguise herself, not wanting anyone to recognize the famous "Queen of Burlesque" at a church service in the mall.

I closed the sermon with something like this:

It was your sins and mine that nailed Jesus to the old rugged cross. But that's not the end of the story, for God the Father raised Him from the dead.

Easter is the celebration of our Lord's resurrection. He defeated death and rose with victory over sin, hell and the grave. Jesus said, "I am the resurrection and the life. He who believes in me will live, even though he dies." *(John 11:25 NIV)*

If you want to receive forgiveness for your sins, if you want to receive Christ into your heart and life, pray this prayer with me now.

Oh God, I know that I am a sinner. You sent Your Son, Jesus Christ to die for me. I want to receive Him in my heart now. Please, dear Lord, forgive me for all my sins and give me the gift of eternal life.

Evelyn explained to me later that she began crying while I was closing the message. Somehow she was able to get the telephone number where I was staying and called me. Still in tears, she invited me to their mansion to tell her more about Jesus.

Preaching in the burlesque joint

While we were visiting, she invited me to preach at the Green Gate Club again and when I accepted, she began immediately to arrange for some publicity.

The news media was there to cover the service as if it was a major league sporting event. Many of the church members were appalled that I would even consider preaching in a burlesque joint; to me it was taking the Gospel to the dregs of society. If anyone on the face of the earth needed the Word it was those folks.

Evelyn made this announcement to the patrons of the club, "there will be no drinks sold and no smoking while the 'Reverend' is speaking. When he finishes you can drink as much as you like."

I wanted the Holy Spirit to touch their lives so they would never want another drink from the cesspool of sin.

We rented Blossom Stadium.

I preached one night in the club, then we moved the services to a Baptist Church that had been praying for a revival. The crowds grew so large we had to rent Blossom Stadium to accommodate everyone. From Blossom Stadium, we moved the crusade to the downtown sports arena where the San Antonio Spurs played basketball.

During the crusade, the Spurs needed the arena for a playoff game. The owner of the team came to me to negotiate for the building. Mind you, it was where they played all their home games, but we had a lease contract and they had to meet our wishes.

This was the deal!

The Spurs had to pay for the rest of our contract on the arena; at half-time I would speak to the crowd about Jesus and the marquee on the Lone Star Beer clock was to read, **"Serving Jesus is fun!"**

While a lot of "Christian" folks looked down their religious noses and were dismayed that I would "lower" my standard to be seen in such a den of iniquity, thousands were being ushered into the Kingdom of heaven. It all happened because the Lord gave me the holy boldness to go where other preachers would not dare.

I love the saying, "Faith marches in where cowards fear to tread!"

During the crusade, I was scheduled to debate Madalyn Murray O'Hare on a television show there in San Antonio. I invited Evelyn to go and sit in the audience. After the debate I introduced the two ladies.

As we left the studio I asked Evelyn for her opinion of the debate and Ms. O'Hare. Her answer was to the point and not very polite. She didn't address the debate but expressed her thoughts of Madalyn.

"You could see hate and frustration in her face and when you looked in her eyes, they were the most vacant, the most devoid of life, I have ever seen."

I have written about Madalyn elsewhere in this book and always considered her a friend; unfortunately, Evelyn's commentary on her was accurate.

In the few moments of personal encounter, the atheist's repugnant spiritual condition had left a definite mark on Mrs. Linton.

Dear God, I'm worse than she is!

Several years later Evelyn related to a radio audience her thoughts as she rode home from the debate and meeting Madalyn Murray O'Hare.

In quiet contemplation of her own life and the woman she had just met, Evelyn said, "Dear God, I'm worse than she is! Her life is a vacuum and so is mine. She's working for the devil and so am I. I have a big Bible at home but I never read it. She denies the very existence of God. I know there is a God but I've never invited His Son to come into my heart to be my Lord and Savior. I'm worse off than she is; I'm the biggest hypocrite in town!"

Even though Evelyn thought of herself as a hypocrite at that moment, she really wasn't one. She was simply a hell bound sinner. She knew about Jesus in the same manner she knew about George Washington. Christ was nothing more than an historical figure that she had heard or read about.

George Washington and his greenback buddies

She was much better acquainted with Washington and his greenback buddies, Abe Lincoln, Andy Jackson, Tom Jefferson and Ben Franklin. She took their pictures with her at all times. They were the ones who provided her with earthly possessions. Since she was without Christ, George and his pals were her dearest friends and her only security.

When we arrived at her home, the weight of conviction was so heavy Evelyn couldn't bear it any longer. She was lost; she knew it and didn't want to be. Inside the house she and Guy knelt at an antique table. It was the one from the home of the Justice of the Peace who married them. They had returned to purchase it from him several years after the marriage ceremony.

It served as an altar for them to be joined together in marriage and it was now the altar where they surrendered their lives to Christ.

I have had the joy of praying the sinner's prayer with thousands of people. None however, was ever more thrilling than when Evelyn and Guy Linton called on Him on April 4, 1970. A pastor and his wife from a local Baptist church were there to witness the miracle of their salvation. We all rejoiced! Nothing on earth produces greater joy in heaven than for sinners to get saved.

It wasn't that Evelyn and Guy were worse sinners than anyone else; it was their measure of influence. To them the greatest thing in the world was money. I wouldn't have been surprised to find the words of a song from the 1950's bronzed and hanging on their wall,

Money

Let me feel it, let me fold it,
Give it to me, let me hold it,
Give me money, money, money, money,
money;
Let me live in regal splendor,
Let me have that legal tender,
Give me money, money, money, money,
money;
Let me have that double eagle,
Give it to me 'cause it's legal,
Give me money, money, money, money,
money!

It isn't wrong to have plenty of money. But the Lintons were so obsessed with it that they cared for nothing else and certainly not for the lives they helped to ruin.

In their school, Evelyn taught five hundred young women a year to take off their clothes in the most seductive manner. Pornography in the Green Gate Club was not pictures; it was bare flesh. They had a simple philosophy, if a smile will get past the cop, that's all you need to wear. Evelyn wanted her girls to be thread bare.

While she never danced or stripped, she was a legend when it came to instructing others. And she did it without remorse, without consideration of the consequences or that she was influencing lives and speeding them toward eternal hell.

The lust lounge

It's no wonder the imps of darkness were so distraught when Evelyn and Guy knelt and confessed Christ as their Savior. The Lintons had made the work of demons a thousand times easier. Their "lust lounge" was a favorite hangout for old Slewfoot himself.

It was not until Christ came into their hearts and washed their sins away that they realized the magnitude of their transgression against the God of heaven and His Son.

Kneeling at the foot of the Cross, they found redemption, total redemption, for it was at the Cross that they gave their sin-stained lives to the Lord and were born again. I recall with vivid memory the inexpressible joy that flooded their lives that day.

Watching them weep and pray brought to mind the words of a wonderful old Hymn of the church.

The cross upon which Jesus died
Is a shelter in which we can hide
And its grace so free is sufficient for me
And deep is its fountain as wide as the sea.

There's room at the cross for you,
There's room at the cross for you,
Though millions have come, there's still room
    for one
Yes there's room at the cross for you.

(Room at the Cross, Ira Stanphill)

Through tear-filled eyes, Guy looked at me an said, "With Christ in my heart there is no way I can continue to operate the club."

The sign read:

Green Gate Club closed forever.
Evelyn and Guy Linton
have given their hearts to JESUS.
See you in church!

Before the clock struck twelve that night, they had an impromptu closing ceremony with Guy telling the strippers and the customers about their new-found faith in the Lord. Someone made a sign and put it on the door.

The Associated Press picked up the story and immediately sent reporters to find out if it were true. It made all the wire services and the news was sent around the world. A friend of theirs read about it in Munich and wrote to see if it was an accurate report.

Until the day Guy Linton died, they traveled together throughout the United States and several other nations sharing the wonderful story of their salvation.

After the Easter Sunrise Service, when Evelyn invited me to their home I decided that was where God wanted me to stay for the rest of my time in San Antonio. Evelyn made the remark to someone later, "Brother Bob came into our home and just loved the hell out of us."

If lives can be trophies, that's what Evelyn and Guy were to me. The change Christ wrought in their hearts was as miraculous as when He saved Mary Magdalene from a life of prostitution in Bible days. The Lintons not only closed the Green Gate Club, they made it a place where the lost could find Christ.

The Gate of Lust changed
to the Gate of Love.

In reality, the Green Gate Club was nothing more than a Gate of Lust issuing one way tickets to hell. But when Christ came into their lives, it became a Gate of Love through which men and women passed on their journey to heaven. The club became a center for street ministry.

News of my going astray hurt the Lintons deeply but they never gave up hope for my return to the ministry. Although I was away for several years, whenever anyone spoke an unkind word about me, Evelyn was quick to remind them of a man called Peter, who, on the night of Christ's betrayal, denied that he knew Him and cursed His precious name.

"I won't give up on him," she would say, "any more than Christ gave up on Simon Peter. In the depth of my heart I know the Lord will help Brother Bob find his way back home where he belongs."

A big dose of self-importance

How could I do it? How could I ever go back to a life of sin after seeing such marvelous conversions as the Lintons?

I'll tell you how!

Instead of busting out at the seams for Christ, I was busting out of my britches with self-importance. And I was not accountable to anyone.

Self-importance is a sinister evil which has plagued ministers since the days of the early church. With self-importance comes the feeling of invincibility. I had no peers, no one with whom to share my fears or my failures.

I was an island, a world unto myself. The only people on my island were those whom I invited. Anyone else was an intruder and, as a result, when temptation came my way I had no one to help me fight. I had surrounded myself with "yes" people, not prayer warriors.

To engage in spiritual warfare, you must have those who know how to pray, touch heaven, tug at the heartstrings of God and persevere until the answer comes.

If I had asked the namby-pambys who made up my circle of power to pray, they would have recited the used up, worn out, unscriptural one they learned as a child, "Now I lay me down to sleep."

Conceited? Not me!

Some people have a problem with conceit, not me. In my opinion conceited people think they are good. I was long past that—I knew I was!

I was warned of what was happening, both in my spirit and by others. But self-importance has a way of anesthetizing its victim to keep them wrapped in their own little world of "Me-ism." All I ever needed was one more drink from the bottle of self-admiration to keep me intoxicated on me

As I walked out of a television studio following my last debate with Madalyn Murray O'Hare, a former employee of mine came to me and said, "I see 'Ichabod' written across your forehead."

He was saying the glory of the Lord had departed from my life.

Yes, I was warned, but I paid no attention to the Holy Spirit or to those whom He sent. I was going to do my own thing if it hair-lipped the governor.

In my own mind, I could do no wrong, and so what if I did, God would forgive me. After all, I was doing things for Him that no one else had ever done. Since the day that Bourbon Street had been dedicated to the hordes of hell, who had dared to walk amidst its

147

filth with a Bible in hand and confront the war lords of the abyss? I was the only person with the guts to do it. At least that's what I thought.

Each sin has a consequence.

I was right about one thing, God, the eternal, loving God of heaven would forgive me of all the wrongs I was doing because that's His nature, but for each sin there is a consequence.

Let me share a story to emphasize this truth!

In southern Alabama, a wonderful godly family had a son who was rebellious. At an early age, he began causing his mother and dad grief with the things he did. At first, the dad thought he could punish the boy and keep him on the right path but after numerous severe strappings it was obvious to them the young man was incorrigible. They feared that he would end up in prison or, worse yet, be killed in a brawl.

One evening, when the young man came home he noticed a post standing in the middle of the yard. When he asked what it was for, his father said, "Come with me." On their way from the house he noticed his dad picked up a hammer and a sack of nails.

"I'm going to make you a deal," the father said, "there will be no more yelling or strappings for the things you do if you make me a promise. For each wrong deed, you will drive a nail in the post."

"Wait," the boy replied, "you mean no more punishment of any sort, no matter what I do?" "All I have to do is drive a nail in this silly old post? You better have lots of nails!"

The Mom and Dad watched the boy they loved so deeply make his daily trip to the post to drive nails. It was an especially sad day when they saw him go to the post and realize there was no place to drive even one more nail.

The young man stood looking at the post for a long time. He wasn't searching for an empty spot to drive a nail; he was bewildered that he could have done so many evil deeds.

When he came into the house he said to his father, "the deal was that I would drive a nail every time I did something wrong. Will it be okay if I pull one out each time I do something good?"

"You've got a deal," his dad replied. It was as if the young man had been transformed. He set out feverishly to right the wrongs he had done. Where he had once made daily trips to the post to drive nails, he was now on a mission to remove them.

At last the day came when he approached the post to pull out the last nail. From the window where they watched him drive the nails, his mom and dad witnessed the last one being extracted from the post. Thinking they would see him turn around with a big grin on his face, they couldn't understand when his shoulders began to shake and it was obvious he was weeping.

His dad came to where he was standing, put his hand on the young man's shoulder and said, "I thought you would be pleased with yourself when this day finally arrived, son. You have succeeded in pulling out every nail from the post."

"Yes," he said, "the nails have all been removed, but look at all the ugly scars."

Self-importance is
self-destruction in disguise.

That young man's story brought back memories of the wrongs, the transgressions of my own life. With reckless abandon I drove nails in my post. It was not until later that I became cognizant that the nails I was driving were piercing the hands and feet of the Son of God. For my post was the Old Rugged Cross where Jesus suffered, bled and died. My heart broke when I realized my sins were against Christ. There is a verse from the Psalms which sums up my wrong doings.

> Against you, you only, have I sinned and done what is evil in your sight.... *(Psalm 51:4)*

Had it not been for His everlasting love and grace, my self-importance would have led me to self-destruction. The sins in my life made me want to die. My shame pushed me to the brink of eternity. I needed God, O how I needed Him, even though I had forsaken Him and acted as if I didn't need His love any more.

> I've wandered far away from God:
> Now I'm coming home;
> The paths of sin too long I've trod:
> Lord, I'm coming home.
>
> Coming home, coming home,
> Nevermore to roam;
> Open wide Thine arms of love:
> Lord, I'm coming home.
>
> *(Lord, I'm Coming Home,*
> *William J. Kirkpatrick)*

Sin is cancer to the soul.
Shame is cancer to the emotions.

His grace carried me to the mountain of glory, then self-importance drove me to the valley of shame, and there I would have died had it not been for His love. Sin is cancer to the soul, in like manner, shame is cancer to the emotions.

How does anyone recover from such devastation? Is it possible for a person who has known the Lord to fall so completely into sin and depravity and come back? Shame says "no." God says "YES!"

I knew Him. I had received Him as my personal Savior in that little Baptist Church in Sweet Water, Alabama. His wondrous blood had cleansed me from my sin. No one who knew me prior to my conversion could doubt that I had been born again. My life was as different as night and day.

Make me feel good.

When I fell, I became so full of self-gratification, so money-hungry, so power-oriented, nothing else mattered. Not lost souls, not Bourbon Street, not helping hookers to get free, not showing drug addicts the Way, nothing but those things which elevated me and made me feel good.

My life lost all meaning. Bob Harrington was a mere shell of the vibrant, outgoing, sin-hating, devil-disturbing, Christ-exalting, Spirit-anointed man the world knew as The Chaplain of Bourbon Street.

When I reached the bottom and could go no farther, I wanted to curl up and die. I remembered where I came from and longed for the touch of God on my life again. Shame tried to tell me I had sinned so much that not even God could love me. If I had listened to the voice of shame today my remains would be buried in an unmarked grave. The voice of shame, however, was no match for God's strong voice of love and forgiveness. As He forgave Adam, Abraham, Moses, David and Jonah in the Old Testament, Peter and the other deserters in the New, He forgave me and filled me afresh with His Spirit.

Having washed from me the foul stench of the hog wallow, He clothed me again with the garment of praise and renewed a right spirit in me.

Dipping his pen in the inkwell of inspiration, the composer of a beautiful old hymn wrote the story of my redemption,

Jesus paid it all, All to Him I owe;
Sin had left a crimson stain,
He washed it white as snow.

(Jesus Paid It All, Elvina M. Hall)

I left the mountain top of glory and squandered precious years in the valley of shame. The valley of shame is only one step from the valley of the shadow of death but I didn't take up residence there. The Christ, who first loved me and gave Himself for my sins, took me by the hand and led me from the valley. By His grace I am daily living with...

"SUCCESS OVER SHAME!"

Create in me a clean heart, O God,
And renew a steadfast spirit within me.
Do not cast me away from Your presence,
And do not take Your Holy Spirit from me.

Restore to me the joy of Your salvation,
And uphold me by Your generous Spirit.
Then I will teach transgressors Your ways,
And sinners shall be converted to You.

(Psalm 51:10-13 NKJV)

Amen

Chapter Eight

Stunted by Shame

One of my mother's favorite sayings was, "If you smoke and drink, it will stunt your growth!" I came into the world as an eleven pound, twelve ounce baby and grew to be six feet one inch tall, weighing two hundred and fifty pounds. Just think; if I hadn't smoked and drank, I may have been nine feet four inches!

To look at me, you would never think my growth was stunted. In the physical it probably wasn't, but I can tell you, for certain, it was in the spiritual, partially by those very things Mother warned me not to do.

The night I walked down the aisle of the Sweet Water Baptist Church and gave my heart to the Lord, He lifted me up on cloud nine and held me there for a while. How long, I can't say.

This much I know, it was long enough for Him to flush the sin out of my soul and fill me with heavenly peace. When my feet touched the ground again I felt like running to the ends of the earth to tell what He had done for me. In those early years of ministry, pastors would say of me, "he's young, green and growing." That was much better than later when I was "old, ripe and rotten."

I cannot, and will not, compare my life with that of other ministers or draw a conclusion about where I could have been or what the Lord could have done in my life. I came to a crossroad and took the wrong one.

Standing at the crossroads.

I heard a song written by someone under the inspiration of the Holy Spirit.

Standing at the crossroads,
the choice is mine to make;
One goes right, the other left,
which one will I take?
One is straight and narrow;
the other way is broad,
Will I take the right way?
It's the one that leads to God.

During those first years of ministry if a person could be too "holy" I was. Nothing appealed to me except the perfect will of God. My sole purpose in life was to serve the Master and win the lost to Him.

It was inconceivable to me that a man or woman would call themselves Christian and not have a burden for the lost. In my mind I carried a picture of the suffering Christ. It was not the pretty picture you often see of a man with a few sprinkles of blood on His hands and feet or some insignificant welts on His body where He had been beaten. No! No! No! I saw the humiliated Redeemer.

God's sacrificial lamb

The picture in my mind was that of a man being sacrificed as one would an animal. Blood flowed from the crown of thorns He wore, down His face, around the sides of His nose and in the corners of His mouth. His beard was matted with blood, sweat, tears and saliva where the taunting crowd had spit in His face.

His back was a bleeding mass of raw flesh from the chastisement in Pilate's judgment hall. His hands, those precious hands that touched the fevered brow of Simon Peter's mother-in-law, the blind, the lame, and the lepers were pierced by nails.

I carried in my mind a picture so vivid, so alive and so graphic that I wanted everyone to know the full price He paid for our salvation.

How could anyone not want to win the lost if they understood what it cost the Lord to bring salvation into the world? I broke it down this way in my elementary thinking.

It cost Him His place at the right hand of the Father. Yes, He gave up the throne room in heaven, the angelic choir and the streets of gold to come to earth.

Then He gave up His life on earth! Everyone should keep this powerful truth in mind. At any moment during His trial, the beating, the crucifixion, and to the very moment of His death, He could have summoned ten thousand angels to come and deliver Him from the hands of sinful men. He could have come down from the cross. He could have destroyed Pilate, the Roman army, the religious leaders, the world; yes, even the universe with a single word had He chosen to do so. Rather than do any of those things, He elected to die for the sins of the world.

The Cross

He stayed on the cross though they shouted
come down,
He stayed there for you and for me;
As the sacrifice Lamb He came to the earth,
and died on the old rugged tree.

The price He paid was too great for a man,
The price cost heaven its best;
Once for all He put away sin,
The Savior stood the test.

On the lonely hill called Mt. Calvary,
The King of Kings hung suspended;
He touched not the earth or the heavens,
There on the cross His life ended.

The story did not end when He cried it is
finished,
For the crucified Christ rose again;
When the stone was rolled back by the angel,
The soldiers watched but in vain.

He is not here, said the angel,
Come see the place where He lay;
Then go tell the disciples and Peter,
He will meet you on the way.

Centuries have passed since that fateful day,
When the Savior died on the tree;
No greater love has the world ever known,
Than that which He gave you and me."

And it cost him his dignity.

Let me explain!

Jesus was the epitome of a dignified gentleman. He always conducted Himself with utmost grace and godliness. The pictures we see of Him on the cross have a loin cloth around His hips, but in all likelihood, He was naked. As part of the humiliation of crucifixion the Romans denied even a loin cloth to the dying.

When He was crucified Christ was stripped of His clothing.

He was not without emotion when He hung on the cross, the Bible declares that Jesus **"despised the shame"** yet, He endured the terrible travesty that He might pay the price of salvation for all mankind.

162

In those early days of ministry I could not imagine, nor can I now, why men and women would be hesitant to tell anyone and everyone about the wonderful grace of God. My life was so radically changed. I knew I had passed from death to life. The joy of knowing Christ Jesus as my own personal Savior was real and I wanted the world to know Him. I was certain if He could redeem a worthless sinner like me, His love and forgiveness would work for the vilest person who ever walked on planet earth.

My ministry was marked, distinguished, characterized by the desire to win the lost to Christ. In humility I sought Him. His Word was a lamp to my feet and a light to my pathway and prayer was a daily necessity for my soul's well being.

I'm talking about real prayer, when a man or woman agonizes before the throne of God. Soul-searching, gut-wrenching prayer that can sweep away the clouds of an overcast sky and bring the sunshine of God's love streaming through. Not the kind of prayer that has become popular today which is little more than a cheap bargaining session.

The golden arches prayer

Too many people pray like Farmer McDonald's wife. You remember, "Old McDonald had a farm, and on his farm he had a wife. With a gimme, gimme here and a gimme, gimme there!" God is not running a heavenly "M" with drive thru service.

If all an individual needs is a burger and fries, then they should go to the nearest drive-in, but that's not what my heart cried for. I wanted to win the lost at any cost. I longed to invade the palaces of darkness with the light of life. Just as I had done with Evelyn and Guy Linton, I wanted to "love the hell" out of every sinner I met and the only way to do it was to seek the face of God daily.

Destiny is measured by courage.

Where does a man or woman get courage? As a child, I got it from fear. The fear of being laughed at by fellow students caused me to do some things I would have never tried otherwise. As an adult, the fear of failure drove me to accomplish feats beyond my abilities. And like a multitude of others, I got a lot of my courage from a bottle.

It is amazing how many people go through life depending on drugs and alcohol to give them the courage to face another day. Sadly, fear, drugs and alcohol do not produce lasting courage, rather a false bravado that fades in the face of strong opposition.

True courage is a quality of mind and temperament that enables a man or woman to remain steadfast when they encounter danger or hardship.

Prayer was not the source of my indomitable courage; prayer was the catalyst that brought me in contact with my Source—Christ Jesus.

Before I was a powerful "man of the cloth" I was a man of dedicated prayer. I knew I was never less alone than when alone with the Lord. We had sweet communion and rich fellowship in those times.

I lived the song,

> He speaks and the sound of His voice,
> Is so sweet the birds hush their singing;
> And the melody that He brings to me,
> Within my heart is ringing;
> And He walks with me, and He talks with me,
> And He tells me I am His own;
> And the joys we share as we tarry there,
> None other has ever known.
> *(In the Garden, C. Austin Miles)*

Life had meaning and purpose because I was committed to the cause of Christ. In those days if you could have dissected my brain you would have found the name of the Lord stamped on every page.

Holy boldness for a heavenly vision

Even though the rapture hadn't occurred I was already caught up. My mind, my thoughts, my goals, aspirations and dreams were to do the will of God. His will was all that mattered. I had a special endowment of holy boldness to accomplish a heavenly vision.

For anyone engaged in cause and effect, my life would have made an excellent case study. The more dedicated I became to the Lord, the greater He worked through me. That, my friend, is cause and effect to the max.

In one of my seminary classes or somewhere I heard a statement made by Dwight L. Moody, a mighty soldier of the cross, "It remains yet to be seen what God will do through the life that is totally dedicated to Him."

Let me be that man.

From the moment I heard those words I wanted to be that man. I wanted to be so dedicated to Christ, so driven by the heavenly vision that nothing, not money, not fame, not women, not pleasures or sins or vices could distract me from His holy call on my life.

There were three distinguishing words that fit and described me in those days—

Commitment

Audacity

Humility

Soul-winning was my game.

A fire raged in my heart. I had a white-hot passion for the lost. I was committed to do whatever it took to win them to the Master. The hour was never too late or too early, the weather was never too bad or the storm too great. Soul-winning was the name of my game, my only game.

My commitment to Christ helped me to turn away from anything that had the appearance of wrong. As long as I continued to read the Word and seek His face daily I stayed committed. The combination of Bible study and prayer kept the flame glowing in my soul.

When I say I had audacity, I'm talking about the positive application of the word. I had a forwardness about me that wouldn't take no for an answer if I knew God was leading me. I had no problem believing the Lord would fulfill each and every one of His promises.

It was not my nature to sit around wishing something good would happen. I remember the advice of a judicious teacher. He said, "Nothing is automatic, you have to make it happen!"

I found the saying true in the business world and when working for the Lord. Sitting on the stool of "do-nothing" gets you nothing; even a turtle has to stick his neck out if he's going to get somewhere. Every time I ventured out in faith the Lord was standing beside me. Never once did He let me down.

That's when I discovered an amazing secret, He expected me to do only what was natural for me and when I did, I could expect Him to do what was natural for Him.

Here's the secret:
what was natural for Him
was supernatural for me.

Once that marvelous truth invaded my soul I stopped trying to do His job. It made it much easier to concentrate on the work He wanted me to do.

My job was to preach the Gospel, love the sinners and win them to Christ. It was His responsibility to save, forgive and write the names in the Book of Life. I was audacious enough to believe He couldn't spell their name correctly.

Humility? Most of my friends never thought of me and humility at the same time. Yet, it was one of my strong points in the early years of my ministry.

Before I go any farther with what some will think is a charade, let me clarify humility. It doesn't mean to be down in the mouth, defeated, stepped on by the devil and anyone else who cares to try. It isn't "PMS," "Poor Me Syndrome," or tears in my ears from lying on my back crying over lost love or woe is me!

Meekness is not weakness!

The true meaning of the word is harnessed strength. Moses, the Bible said, was the meekest man on the earth, yet no one thought of him as being weak.

Both Jesus and Moses were meek but not weak

Speaking with a quiet voice, or just above a whisper, does not mean a person is meek. Moses spoke to three million people at a time. Jesus taught multitudes and neither of them had the luxury of a microphone or a speaker system. They were meek but not weak!

In humility of mind and heart, I sought the Lord and, when I knew the direction He was leading, I was gung-ho to follow Him. In those days I wasn't leaning on my own strength or man's wisdom, because I knew I couldn't make it unless He led the way.

Humility was knowing the work He had for me to do was bigger than I could do alone. I knew that without Him I could never accomplish all He had planned for my life.

So where did I go wrong?

As long as I maintained my commitment, audacity and humility before the Lord, I grew by leaps and bounds. But when I was too busy to study the Bible, let other things crowd into my prayer time and found the pleasures of life more important than telling men and women about salvation my spiritual growth became stunted. I not only stopped growing, but regression set in. All too soon, I was doing the things He saved me from years before. I learned the hard way; there is no place in God for standing still or marking time. You are either going forward or you'll start losing ground faster than a hound chasing a rabbit.

When God saved me I was a mess. Sin had such total dominion over my life that I was like a puppet on the end of the devil's string. He pulled the strings and I danced to please him. I had a filthy mouth, because I had a dirty heart.

In Alabama we didn't use flowery words like "cursed and swore," we cussed! And believe me, I was a "cusser." I took my mother, father, brother, son (even though I didn't have one) and the Lord's name in vain daily. I talked about hell as if it was the next town down the road and I was the only person in our neck of the woods who could give the directions on how to get there.

When I broke fellowship with Him, I returned to my old ways but it wasn't the same. Before I did it out of ignorance—I was a sinner through-and-through—so the things I said and did were the words and deeds of a lost man. This time I knew better.

Prior to knowing Him as my Savior, I took His name in vain and never gave it a second thought. It wasn't so easy the next time around. When I started to say vulgar or filthy words they stuck in my throat like a fish bone.

Hold your hand over your heart.

Standing on the stage of the Green Gate Club, I asked the people to hold their hand over their heart and challenged them to consider what it would mean if their heart stopped beating right then. The people who heard me speak were impacted by those words. Many of them turned their life over to Christ months later because the challenge stayed with them.

There were many nights when that thought invaded my mind, as warped as it was, and sent cold chills running up my spine.

For me, to return to my old life was unthinkable. I knew the Truth; it had set me free from the bondage of sin. My testimony of God's grace had touched thousands of lives around the world.

Don't you know the devil and his imps laughed for glee when they heard me using gutter language again? My mother would have washed my mouth with lye soap if she had heard the things I was saying.

It wasn't just my mouth. The old Bob Harrington, the sinner, the lying, cheating, woman chasing Bob that Christ saved and delivered was trying to be resurrected from the pit. And he almost made it, except, life in sin after I had known the Lord is not the same as it was before. Nothing was as good as it had been. Not that it was so outstanding the first time, but after I had tasted the heavenly gift, it was impossible for sin to satisfy the hunger of my soul. I longed for the water of life and nothing else could slake my thirst.

To say I was miserable would be the understatement of the century!

I really thought money would do the trick so I set out to make as much as I possibly could.

To my chagrin, I discovered that money, in and of itself, cannot produce contentment. Whether I had large sums or none at all I was unhappy, because without my daily dose of fellowship with Christ I was unfulfilled. My life was as empty as last year's bird's nest.

From childhood I was always full of energy, looking to the next day, the next mile, the next goal. I was a super achiever, never accepting defeat and certainly never quitting. I had never faced anything quite like this before. There was simply nothing left in me.

The golden cord of fellowship with Christ was broken and I had nothing from which to draw life and strength. I was nothing more than a shell of the man God meant for me to be. When I looked in the mirror I didn't like the person I saw. I had become a stranger to my own eyes.

Shame clawed at my heart and reduced me to a shadow of the once strong, vigilant soldier of the cross I had been. The dreams and visions that once motivated me to higher heights now danced like a mirage on a distant horizon.

There was no hope in my spirit, no joy in my heart, no peace in my soul. I was a man condemned on shame's death row. One of the tragedies of shame is that death is delayed as long as possible to make the victim suffer endlessly. Shame never sleeps or takes a day off. When it has a person in its grip, the torment never stops.

Shame tried to convince me that the Lord would not forgive me because He no longer loved me. It assured me that I was a "has been" and nothing could ever resurrect the high call of God in my life again.

Shame led me to the point, the brink, the very edge of self-destruction. I was so close to ending the drudgery of what my life had become.

I was this close!

From my hotel room on the seventh floor, I looked at the street below and said, "This is high enough to do the job. I won't survive a plunge like that."

Inside my head there was a voice urging me on, "open the window and jump; your sorrows will be over and you won't go on hurting others. Jump...JUMP... **JUMP**!"

I was jolted back to reality from the almost hypnotic trance by the ringing of the telephone in my room.

Who on earth would be calling me?

No one knew where I was and I had not asked the front desk to get anything for me. Who on earth would be calling me?

The answer is plain and simple; it was God! Oh, I don't mean the Lord was on the other end of the line when I answered the phone; the voice I heard was that of the dearest friend a man could ever have, Rex Humbard. The message, however, was straight from the heart of God.

"Brother Bob, you've been away too long; it's time to come home."

"Rex, how did you find me?" I asked, "No one knows where I am!"

"As I was praying, the Lord spoke to my heart to call you. Obviously, He knows where you are," he said.

My conversation with my friend Rex didn't last very long; I had some urgent business to take care of. I had to get my heart ready; it was time to go home.

In years gone by, I had led multiplied thousands in a prayer of repentance. Now it was time for me to follow the advice I had so freely given. The bed in that hotel room made a wonderful altar. I knelt beside it and prayed a prayer that went something like this.

Dear Jesus, forgive me of my sins. I know I have failed You, disappointed You and I have no one to blame but myself.

I have gone astray from Your love and mercy. I have ignored Your voice when You spoke to me and have continued to break Your heart. I'm sorry Lord! Forgive me. Wash me again in Your precious blood and make me clean.

Dear God, You are my only hope; without You I am doomed to continue in this misery. I'm not worthy of Your love and forgiveness but You had Rex call and tell me it's time to come home to You.

If You will forgive me and take me back I will live the rest of my life for You.

Tears were flowing from my eyes like a torrent. As the tears bathed my face, He bathed my heart, soul and spirit. I stood to my feet a new person.

Shame sought my demise, drove me to the brink of destruction and shouted in my ears that Bob Harrington was forever ruined. But the blood of Jesus Christ, the eternal Son of God, wrote **REDEEMED** all over my name. I realized immediately that I could do nothing about my past but I could do everything about my future. Choice, not chance, determines destiny. My future was not about my past; that was over, dead and buried. What lay ahead was a brand new start and a glorious finish.

A human agent on a divine assignment.

The call of God had never been lifted from my heart. He had called me, a human agent, and sent me on a divine assignment. I'm convinced that He knew me as He did King David in Bible times, before I was ever born. He knew the wrong path I would take. He was aware of every sin I committed and He knew I would come back to Him.

Did the Lord overlook my sins? Absolutely not! He neither overlooked nor excused them. He forgave them! I had to be cleansed of my sins. He had to wash me in His sacrificial blood. He didn't condone the things I did because I was special to Him. He forgave me because He is God and He wants to forgive every sinner.

Did shame sneak off into a corner like a whipped dog and die? Not on your life! It fought like a wildcat to keep me in its clutches. Even today it tries to rear its ugly head and put me back on death row but I refuse to be bound by its lies. I'm redeemed, set free, alive again and going stronger than ever for God. I am no longer stunted by Shame. I'm growing everyday with...

"SUCCESS OVER SHAME!"

Eternal God of heaven,
the God whose grace and mercy
extends beyond time and space,
whose marvelous love
transcends all that we can ask or think.

Look down from Your majestic throne
and see the needs of Your people.
Hear the cries of each man, woman and child
who calls on You with a humble heart.
In Jesus name, Amen.

Chapter Nine

Shame Brings Condemnation. Freedom Comes from Grace.

Celebration, with a capital **C**! That's the best way I know to describe what happened to me when the Lord Jesus came into my heart and set me free. He washed my sins in His precious blood and started a celebration in my life.

I stated earlier in this book I was not a goody-goody sinner; sin was my favorite activity. It wasn't something I did to idle the time away; I was serious about my sinful lifestyle. I found great pleasure in wickedness.

This is why the change in my life was so drastic. The people who knew me as a sinner couldn't help but notice what the Lord had done.

When the celebration of salvation started in my life, it totally enveloped my being. Not only did Bob Harrington get saved, everything around him got saved. My actions, my thoughts, my desires, my behavior and my language were all refashioned. The Scripture promises:

> Therefore, if anyone is in Christ, he is a new creation; old things have passed away; behold, all things have become new.
>
> (II Corinthians 5:17 NKJV)

The new birth, the newness of life that flowed into my heart when Christ transformed me, was a complete work of grace. I wasn't just redeemed inwardly; His redemption worked on the outside as well. I walked, talked, ate, drank, dressed, and smelled like a convert of the Lord's.

A warrior's spirit

I quickly realized that being saved personally was not enough. I wanted everyone I came in contact with to know the sweet love of Jesus. God gave me a warrior's spirit and sent me out to win the lost to Him.

One of my friends likened me to an old German who found the Lord late in life. His salvation was so wonderful, so miraculous and so fulfilling, the old man told everyone he could find about Christ.

Some of the men in the town where the old man lived thought it would be fun to introduce this new Christian to an avowed atheist. No sooner had the two shook hands than the old German began testifying of God's grace in his life. To this the atheist replied, "Sir, I don't even believe there is a God."

Without a moment's hesitation, the old man said, "The Bible tells us, 'the fool says in his heart, there is no God,' but you be the biggest fool I ever did see; you blabber it right out!"

Divine heartburn

My heart was aflame with the desire to lead men and women to Christ right from the start. The divine heartburn never stopped regardless of where I went or what I did. From the moment He washed and cleansed me the longing and hunger to see broken lives mended was always with me.

I understand the euphoria a doctor experiences when he has labored for hours in an operating room and at last emerges smiling because the life-saving surgery was a success.

I know the exhilaration an athlete feels when he has won a major event, or the excitement of the checkered flag when the winning driver crosses the finish line at the Indianapolis 500. All of those emotions burst forth in my heart when I see the lost come to Christ.

The Bible declares that heaven erupts with rejoicing when a sinner repents. To me, nothing, absolutely nothing, on earth can equal the thrill of that moment.

If we ever recognize the vast potential God has placed inside each of us we will become living dynamos for Christ.

We are not a bunch of defeated outcasts. We are not misfits in a sophisticated world of do-gooders. We are the salt of the earth, we are the light of the world. We house the hope for any tomorrow this universe may have.

We can change the world.

The children of God are the last bastion of freedom for all creation. We have the wonderful distinction of being the only entity on earth that can change the world. We can do it if we will!

I was a candidate to try anything that would attract the lost to Christ. That's why the chapel on Bourbon Street appealed to me. It was something nobody else thought would work. It had a measure of danger and the challenge was enough to keep me going at a fevered pace.

Few people know the real Bourbon Street. I didn't, until I walked it day after day, week after week, month after month and year after year.

Nothing less than eternity will reveal the tragic losses that have occurred on America's number one boulevard to hell.

Walk with me down the street and let me point out some of the dives where bodies are sold like slaves in an open market. Step inside the dens of iniquity with me and you will see sin at its filthiest. Your ears will hear the foul sounds of the demon possessed and your nostrils will be assaulted by the fumes from the opium and cocaine parlors. No street on earth is like this. Blood mixed with booze and the secretions of human bodies flow unchecked. This twelve-city block piece of real estate rivals the ancient cities of Rome, Babylon, Athens and Sodom and Gomorrah where sin, sex and perversion were the rage of the day. It is lewd, vulgar and contemptible to the Lord God Jehovah.

An angel
with the sword of vengeance

Believe me, while judgment is overdue, God has not forgotten. The angel of death will come with a swift sword of vengeance. He will annihilate, wreck, devastate and destroy this once proud city whose destiny has long since been decided.

Not far from the "Chapel on Bourbon Street" was the late Al Hirt's place. Al was loved by millions of people around the world, many of them Christians who thought because he played "When The Saints Go Marching In" so beautifully on the trumpet, he had to know the Lord.

I won't demonize the man nor judge where his soul is at this moment, but you need to know, sin ruled in the "king of the trumpeters' " establishment. His place was known as a hooker's hangout. Homosexuality, lesbianism, booze, coke, speed and all other kinds of illegal drugs were as prevalent as water.

Al was known to associate with various ministers from time to time. Sadly, those with whom he chose to hob-knob were not driven by a passion to win the lost so they never made him feel uncomfortable about sin.

Close to Al Hirt's place was one of the seediest joints on planet earth. It's hard to describe the unmitigated filth on the floor alone. You can't imagine how many drunks trudged into that place day and night with too many drinks under their belts. They would get sick and regurgitate. But nobody cleaned up the mess. The mindless crowds would shuffle through the repulsive stench and go on like sheep to the slaughter.

It was considered one of the lower class places, the strippers there were not the young beautiful girls right out of high school. They were the older age group— twenty-five to thirty years old. Their faces and bodies showed they were used up by drugs, prostitution and liquor.

Stringy headed and snaggle-toothed victims

A man had to be terribly drunk or totally out of his mind to find the "ladies" in the "Hotsy-Totsy Club" attractive. Their teeth had either rotted away from drugs or a pimp, or some other abusive man had knocked them out. In most instances their hair looked as if they combed it with an egg beater. The few times I was close enough to smell their breath it was about the same as the floor I described earlier.

These women were so desperate for drugs or booze, they would allow the men who bought them to do anything they pleased. It was not uncommon to find them dead after being brutalized by one or more of the pleasure-crazed, kinky, freaks who frequented that hell hole.

Do you have the stomach for me to show you some of the nicer places?

The next ones are known as the "silk stocking" area of the French Quarter.

I'll open the doors and let you look inside. Except for the thick pale of smoke, these are nothing like the place I described earlier. These are the places where the more "refined" people go. At the bar, you see the beautiful young, very young, ladies.

If you ask one her age, she will tell you she is twenty-one. She will even have ID to prove it but you can rest assured it was provided by the unscrupulous vermin who is turning her into a tramp.

Runaways are prime
targets for pimps.

The scene I'm about to describe is repeated over and over again in cities throughout America but more especially in New Orleans.

A young boy or girl steps off the bus with no place to go, nothing to eat and no money in his or her pocket. When they ran away from home they couldn't have known the dangers or pitfalls which lay ahead. In most instances, they simply wanted to escape an overbearing mother or an abusive father.

These young people are immediately "befriended" by a pimp who has polished his guise until he is totally believable. He gives them money, furnishes a place to stay, feeds them and, most importantly, listens to their sad story.

It isn't that he is interested in them as an individual; he is weaving a web around them that will eventually destroy their life. Pimps are blood sucking parasites. They have only one objective—make slaves of the innocent and unsuspecting children who fall prey to him.

Less than two weeks

The time it takes the average "white slaver" to turn a virgin into a prostitute is usually less than two weeks. Think of that for a moment; a naïve young person ruined for life in little more than the blink of an eye. And the tragedy never seems to end.

By the time you see the young people in the "high class" places, the die is cast. They are already enslaved to some illegal drug and they have begun their journey down the long corridors of darkness.

Once you get past the fluff and facade, you realize how very wicked and depraved the real Bourbon Street is.

The Bible tells us Jesus wept over the city of Jerusalem. I'm sure He has done the same for New Orleans, especially the French Quarter. It was His broken heart that led me to open the "Chapel on Bourbon Street."

What was the attraction?

Was it the availability of the warped, twisted, degenerate way of life on Bourbon Street that attracted me? Was there a flaw deep in my emotional makeup that made me want to make that place my headquarters? Was my lower nature the ruling factor in my going to a city so devoid of the Holy Spirit of God?

No! I say this in all humility, when I went to New Orleans my heart was clean and pure before the Lord. I was so full of the Holy Spirit there was no room for the sinful things of the world.

The spirit of lust that had once reigned supreme in my life was dead, buried and powerless. I was God's man from the moment I awakened until I pillowed my head at night. And when I slept, I dreamed of winning every lost soul in the French Quarter to Him.

I adopted this poem as my motto for living:

Only one life, twill soon be past;
Only what's done for Christ, will last.

From the deep recesses of my spirit I knew Jesus loved every hooker, pimp, pill-popping, coke-snorting, heroin-shooting drug addict, every alcoholic, club owner, thief, murderer, mobster, stripper, dancer and wayward child in that infamous city.

He loved them with an everlasting love and when the vision burned in my spirit I loved them too.

My error was that I didn't guard the vision or the fire He kindled in my spirit. When I allowed myself to get involved in sin, the flame dwindled and the coals ceased to glow. My fellowship with God was broken when my heart went astray from Christ.

A man without a vision

The wisest king of the Old Testament said, "Where there is no vision, the people perish."

In my mad search for pleasure I transferred my allegiance from the things of God to the things of the world. I wanted recognition as a man of persuasive powers, one who could lead others to happiness, wealth and success. The thing I had not considered was that my past successes were rooted in the vision of the Lord. Without His daily guidance I became a man without a vision.

My whole life quickly got out of focus. I still had a massive drive. I knew the importance of goal setting and that a person needs to keep daily tabs on where they are in respect to achieving their goals but my formula was not working for me. I tried to be enthused, but something was missing and I couldn't make it work for me.

I had forgotten the words of Dr. Norman Vincent Peale, in his best selling book, "The Power of Positive Thinking."

He said, "When a man questioned me as to why I always talk about God in my courses on positive thinking, I explained to him enthusiasm is translated from the Greek word 'En-Theo' which means, 'full of God'. No one is truly enthused until they get full of God."

Full of Christ
or Bob Harrington's wisdom?

No wonder it worked so well for me when I was being divinely directed. At that time I was trying to get men and women's hearts filled with Christ. As a "motivator," I was simply getting them full of Bob Harrington's wisdom.

Make no mistake about it, the motivational seminars were great for training men and women to be better sales people and stronger leaders on the job. I knew the jargon. I could tell people how to dot every "I" and cross every "T" and that part was fine but it wasn't where God had called me to be. I was not leading the lost to Christ!

When doing spiritual warfare, it is important to remember you are either taking ground or losing it and I was doing the latter. I tried my hand at being Bob Harrington, the guru of the motivational circuit during the week, and God's man on Sunday. I was really trying to straddle the fence, to be a Christian, a preacher and a saint on the Lord's Day and a sinner the rest of the week. I was going to be the "hot-shot" of both worlds.

I don't need to tell you it didn't work. I was as miserable as a hound dog with a family of fleas on its back and a bumble bee sitting on his nose.

I traded dependence for independence.

When my self-declared arrangement didn't work, I simply checked out on Christ; traded my dependency on Him for my "independence." As they say in the south, I became as independent as a hog on ice. Not that one of those has very much value.

With my new found independence, I also opened the door to an old associate of mine—**FEAR**! Not since I gave my testimony the first time in the little Baptist Church in Sweet Water, Alabama, had I been troubled with fear. Now it moved into my life like a long lost friend.

The love of Christ had set me free from fear, but when I opted for an independent lifestyle, and moved away from the covering He provided, I was a sitting duck for that sinister power to enter my life.

One of the writers of the New Testament penned this magnificent statement:

> There is no fear in love; but perfect love casts out fear, because fear involves torment.
>
> *(I John 4:18 NKJV)*

What did I have to be afraid of? In a word—everything! It was as if I became paranoid about my health, my wealth (or the lack thereof), life and death! It's hard to believe that a man who had preached and prayed thousands into heaven would be concerned about death, but I was.

I had always been as healthy as a horse but fear made me think I had tuberculosis every time I came down with a cold. I was certain every ache and pain was cancer or some other dreaded disease.

My friend, the late Dr. John Osteen, said it so beautifully, "through fear, the devil can make you believe a pimple is a life-threatening cancer. If you're not careful, he will have you convinced that you are dying with a heart attack when all you have is a mild case of heartburn."

Here is the sad part. I knew the tricks of the devil and how he fabricates all kinds of lies, but when I chose to live outside the Lord's covering, I became vulnerable to every attack he wanted to bring my way.

By aligning myself with the father of lies, I placed myself at the mercy of the unmerciful. My decision was bad and the consequences were devastating! I took the devil at his word and paid a dear price.

The Indian and
the talking snake

Years ago I read the story of a young Indian who was going through the initiation process of becoming a brave. One of the tests was to climb a high mountain, spend the night alone, and return with the pelt of an animal he had killed and dressed by himself.

When he reached the summit of the mountain he saw a snake, coiled and almost frozen to death. The snake said to the young man, "please, take me down with you; I'm freezing in the cold." "No", replied the young warrior, "if I take you down, you will bite me and I'll die."

"If you just take me down, you will save my life. I'm dying from the cold. I won't bite you," promised the snake.

So the young Indian wrapped the snake in his clothes and began his journey back to the village. As they descended the mountain, the warmth of the clothes and the lower atmosphere rejuvenated the cold, lethargic snake and, true to his nature, he bit the boy.

In anguish, the boy cried out, "you promised you wouldn't bite me if I brought you down." "But you knew I was a snake and you should not have trusted me!"

Like that Indian boy, I believed the lies of a snake. The one I was listening to, however, wasn't a "myth" on a mountain top, he's the same slithering, slimy reptile who lied to Adam and Eve in the Garden of Eden.

What astonishes me is that he has continued his parade of lies for so many generations and people all over the world keep falling for them. Me? I was a gullible sucker. I knew better than to believe him. He is, has always been and will forever be—a liar.

Truth comes from the lips
of Jesus Christ, God's Son!

It's puzzling to me that anyone would believe the mindless, blabbering lies of the devil rather than the truth which comes from the lips of Jesus Christ, God's Son. Lies incarcerate the soul, truth sets men free.

As a keeper of the truth, it was my responsibility to expose the pernicious fakery and falsehoods the enemy was foisting on men and women. I was duty bound to sow truth like a farmer sowing precious seed.

My field to plant the seed of life started out as Bourbon Street, but as I proved faithful, the Lord continued to enlarge my sphere of influence until I was planting the Word across this great land from border to border and coast to coast. I was a talking machine for Christ. Words flowed out of my mouth like a mighty river. I could talk faster than most people could think. It wasn't the speed with which I spoke, however; it was my subject.

I had no creed but Christ,
No law but love,
No book but the Bible!

Then rebellion reared its ugly head in my life again like it did when I was a child. Back then I cried, pouted, stomped my feet and yelled to get my way. As an adult, I was more subtle but it was the same old tune. My parents made the grave mistake of giving in to my tantrums. I assure you, God didn't. He allowed me to have my own way but with this condition, if being my own man meant living outside His blessings, so be it!

While Christ never stopped loving me and was always ready to forgive, He didn't chase after me to part my beard and stuff a pacifier or a bottle in my mouth every time I whimpered. When I said, to God, "I'm on my own and don't need You," He said, "Okay" and let me find out the hard way how much I did need Him.

Wasted years

It was irrational of me to continue the path of rebellion I had chosen. I wasn't three leaps out of the chute until I knew for certain I had made a tragic mistake but I was as bull-headed as a man could get. At that point I told myself I didn't care if I was making a mistake. I was man enough to muscle my way through. I was going to make it work whether God wanted it to or not. That miscalculation cost me nearly seventeen precious soul-winning years. It became my dark ages—wasted years!

Wasted lives

The years I wasted were nothing in comparison to the wasted lives. To begin—my own family! God blessed me with two wonderful daughters whom I loved more than anything on earth. They were a constant source of joy and comfort. They were beautiful, bright, articulate and to me—outstanding. I was proud of them just as they were of their daddy. Through rebellion I wasted myself to them.

But it wasn't just my family that was sadly disillusioned; my departure from the Lord gave the devil a foothold to attack weak Christians wherever the story was told.

Wasted dreams

Have you ever been so close to the fulfillment of a dream you could reach out and touch it? You knew it was there because it was so real, so vibrant, so alive you could bask in its glow? That's how close I was to my greatest ambition when I turned my back on all that was good, right and holy.

All I ever really wanted to be was a soulwinner, a man totally and completely surrendered to God. My dream was that I would be depleted, exhausted, used up, spent and worn out for the Kingdom of God. Sin wasted my dreams!

Condemnation
with a capital K

With waste came shame and with shame a bombardment of diabolical condemnation. At the beginning of this chapter, I said the celebration started in my life from the moment of my salvation—with a capital C. Using that same standard, condemnation is with a capital K, because it's a **Killer**!

There is no way to know how many times I quoted this passage from the Bible:

> There is therefore now no condemnation to those who are in Christ Jesus, who do not walk according to the flesh, but according to the Spirit. *(Romans 8:1 NKJV)*

I had never bothered to look at what happens when an individual is walking after the dictates of the flesh. The Word had already warned that, outside of Christ, the killer, condemnation, lurks like a lion.

My problem was compounded because I was too stubborn to acknowledge my wrong. If God and I were going to have a relationship, it would have to be on my terms. I was the one in control or that's what the devil wanted me to believe. Nothing could have been farther from the truth. I was being manipulated by the sinister powers of darkness.

A song was popular in the sixties, that, had I listened to and given heed to its message, would have saved me a great deal of suffering and grief.

> Wasted years, wasted years O how foolish,
> As you walk on in darkness and fears;
> Turn around, turn around, God is calling,
> He's calling you from a life of wasted years.
> *(Wasted Years, Wally Fowler)*

Shame brought mega-doses of condemnation to me. Even when I did something good I couldn't enjoy it. I was so beaten down by shame I was convinced I was worthless and the world would be a better place without me.

Liberty and freedom are words never associated with shame because shame enslaves every life it touches.

We talk about the days of slavery being over in America but I for one can testify that slavery is as real today as it was prior to the civil war.

The difference in today's slavery and that of those dark despicable years of the past, is men and women now labor under the yoke of spiritual bondage, opposed to the physical servitude alone.

I do not mean to minimize the horrors or the inhumane treatment the African Americans endured during that period of time which left a mark of disgrace on our nation. Slavery is bad whether it is one person owning another or sin and shame owning someone.

No human being could lay claim on Bob Harrington; I was not in anyone's debt. I was a slave first to sin and then to shame! Sin was mine by choice; shame came on its own.

God's wonderful grace is His gift to mankind; He makes no distinction as to race or color of skin. Grace, simply put, is the undeserved favor of the Lord.

I know about grace first hand. His grace found me when I was a lost, hell-bound sinner and brought heaven alive in my heart. And His grace came again when I deserved hell as much as any man who ever lived. I was a traitor to my faith, my calling, family, friends and my God, but He came to me with love and grace. The words of a chorus I heard not long ago describe it so beautifully.

> Amazing grace how sweet the sound,
> Amazing love now flowing down;
> From hands and feet nailed to the tree,
> His grace flows down and covers me.
> *(Grace Flows Down,*
> *David Bell, Louie Giglio & Rod Padgett)*

I toiled under shame's constant abuse. There were moments when the condemnation was so powerful, so unrelenting, it seemed as if I was being sucked down a long mine shaft to the eternal abyss. My life was a bitter, bottomless hole which led to the pit of hell. Shame filled me with such condemnation, it made me feel lower than a snake's belly.

Broken by sin, condemned by shame; despondent of life and fearful of death; I was but a scrap, a fragment, a speck of the man God called me to be. Wrapped in humiliation, shame had taken its final toll, I could go on no farther, it was the end of the line for me. Sin brought shame and shame brought condemnation, but Jesus Christ brought grace wonderful grace, life saving, sin forgiving, shame defeating grace.

The mystery of grace is that God can make the past as if it never happened.

Through His marvelous grace alone I have discovered the secret to living with...

"SUCCESS OVER SHAME!"

Father of grace, mercy and love,
look down on Your children
as we struggle to win the battle
against the forces of evil.

Send Your Holy Spirit
to empower us that we may be
examples of Your wondrous grace
to a lost and dying world. Amen.

Chapter Ten

The Street of Shame

One of the most exciting portions of the Bible is the description of the heavenly city, the "New Jerusalem." For centuries, poets, playwrights and composers have been inspired by its fabled beauty.

We are given a glimpse of the majestic city in the Book of Revelation. John writes of it in such loving terms and describes it as a place beyond the grandest imaginations of mortal man.

By the best calculations we have, the city is fifteen hundred miles long, wide and high. That's fifteen hundred miles cubed. It may not seem very large when all you see is numbers, so let me put it into perspective.

Take a map and make the starting point about fifty miles east of Dallas, Texas. If you go straight north fifteen hundred miles you will be above the Canadian border, turn left and go fifteen hundred miles west. This will take you somewhere in the vicinity of Vancouver, BC. Turn left again and go directly south fifteen hundred miles, you'll be in the Los Angeles area, turn left again and go fifteen hundred miles east, you will be back where you started.

And that's just the ground floor. Don't forget, the New Jerusalem is fifteen hundred miles high.

If you spent twenty four hours on each square mile, you couldn't cover the first floor in six thousand one hundred years. This should give you an idea of how large this wonderful city is.

In the Revelation, John spoke of the streets as being pure gold, so bright, so clean and so lustrous they are like a polished mirror.

Let me draw you a word picture of the streets as I envision them. Each one begins at the throne of the Lord which is in the center of the city and leads out to one of the gates. The Word tells us there are three gates on each wall that means there are twelve gates and twelve resplendent avenues.

These magnificent boulevards are actually divided highways with a river as the center median. It's called the River of Life. The river is lined on each side with the Tree of Life. Did I mention every street is made of solid gold?

Gold—heaven's paving material.

I heard about a man who dreamed he died and went to heaven. While on earth he had managed his assets well and had accumulated a vast fortune. Not long before his death he turned all his resources into gold and was able somehow to take it all with him.

He was met at the gates of the glorious city by none other than Saint Peter. As they talked, Peter noticed the bag the man was carrying. He told him how unusual it was for him to have brought anything from earth with him.

The man proudly responded that he had cashed in all his life's savings before dying and that he had brought it with him. At Peter's request, the man opened his bag. In sheer astonishment, the gate keeper said, "You went to all that trouble to bring paving material?"

When the man awakened he realized how foolish it would be to try to take anything from earth to that wonderful city because God has prepared everything there to perfection.

Our finite minds cannot fathom the beauty and the grandeur which awaits us on the other side of time.

The majestic city not only has streets of gold, it has walls of jasper and the twelve gates are each of one solid pearl. I can't wait to see those "Pearly Gates" but I'd also like to see the oysters that produced such pearls.

Here on earth we've grown accustomed to some common sights that we'll never see in heaven, traffic jams, police cars, fire trucks, hospitals, ambulances, cemeteries, run-down shacks, ghettos, banks, jails, bars and tattoo parlors. I can truthfully say I won't miss any of those things

Mansions, real mansions

It's hard to mention the golden city and not think of the glorious mansions Jesus promised. Throughout the earth there are nice homes, perhaps a few that people might think of as mansions. These are nothing in comparison with those in heaven. Over there we'll have mansions, real mansions.

One of the most ill-fated, short-lived songs of all times was: "Lord Build Me a Cabin in The Corner of Glory Land."

The first time I heard it, I thought to myself, "I don't want a cabin in the corner; I want a mansion on Main Street."

That magnificent city with its unsullied scenery, streets of gold, mansions, the River of Life, flowers that never fade, wilt or die and the majestic throne of God designed and built by the Architect of the ages.

Thus far, we have barely touched on the sense of sight. We need to consider the other four because all five of our senses will be gloriously alive when we get there. We're going to see, hear, taste, smell and feel.

Can you imagine the sounds you will hear in that bright city? The celestial air will be charged with angelic music. If the Mormon Tabernacle Choir raises the hair on the back of your neck when they sing the "Hallelujah Chorus" from Handel's Messiah, what will happen when you hear a choir of a million voices singing praises to the King of kings?

No sad songs.

No more funeral dirges, no sad songs of "tears in my ears from lying on my back crying over you." No lost love or sad dog night songs. And no more earth shaking, ear drum shattering, thump, thump, thumping of some hot-rodder sitting at a signal light.

I don't mean to rain on the young peoples' parades, especially those who think the only music is some squiggly sounding guitar running a decibel race with a bass. Heaven's music will be the sweetest, most refreshing sound their ears have ever heard. The orchestras there will play the purest notes in perfect harmony.

We'll hear the familiar voices of our loved ones who are there waiting for us to arrive. Our immortal hearts will leap for joy when the angel says; "The Lord God Jehovah will see you now."

We're going to have concerts every night and once again we'll hear the great singers of earth, King David playing a stringed instrument and singing Psalms; Mahalia Jackson will give her heavenly rendition of "Sweet Little Jesus Boy." Ethel Waters will thrill the throngs when she sings "His Eye Is On The Sparrow," as will Jack Holcomb with "Amazing Grace," and Red Foley with "Peace In The Valley." Fanny J. Crosby will silence the angelic choir with "Blessed Assurance."

Stuart Hamblin will rock the rafters when he sings "It Is No Secret," and scores of others will sing the songs of redemption. But Sundays will always hold the greatest concerts of all because that's the Lord's day and He will sing His songs of love to you and me.

Laughter will flood the streets.

Music is just one of the sounds we will hear. Laughter is another. Oh yes, the streets of that wonderful city will be filled with the laughter of children at play.

We'll talk to Daniel about his night in the lion's den and find out what it felt like to sleep among those hungry pussy-cats.

The three Hebrew children will relate to us their sterling performance in the fiery furnace.

Noah will tell us all about the flood; the first bolt of lightning to ever streak across the sky and how frightened the people were when the first thunder boom rolled across the heavens.

I'm sure Jonah has a whale of a story that a lot of folks have found a bit fishy.

Some things we won't hear (and what a blessing that will be). No loud cursing or coarse jokes. No yapping dogs at midnight. No squawking hens at daybreak and no gossiping tongues to disturb our peace. No bombs bursting or bullets whizzing by our heads. No screeching brakes, wailing sirens or sad farewells.

I'll hear my darling mother's voice once more. I'll get to talk to my only son for the first time. (He died at birth.) I'll tell him how much I love him and what a joy it would have been to watch him grow up.

There is one sound, however, that I want to hear more than any other, the voice of my Redeemer when He says, "Well done, good and faithful servant." *(Matthew 25:21)*

A few years ago when I lost my way, had I met Him face to face, He could not have said "Well done" because I was not a good or faithful servant.

Sin tarnished my halo, clipped my wings, took the spring out of my step and the song out of my heart. One of my friends told me later, "I wasn't nearly as worried about you getting your robe over your wings as I was you getting your halo over your horns."

Did you ever wake up on a spring morning and smell the refreshing aroma of honeysuckle? Do you know the sweetness of apple blossoms when the trees are in full bloom? Have you ever been downwind when an orange or lemon tree is in bloom?

Nothing can be more intoxicating to the sense of smell than the fragrance of a rose.

The Ruler of the universe created beautiful odors.

God in His gracious goodness included smelling as one of the five senses which make life on earth so beautiful. The Ruler of the universe took great delight in creating the diverse smells, from tiny flowers to the giant redwoods, from grasses to shrubs, from fruits and vegetables to the spices we use daily.

Can you imagine what it will be like when we walk beside the River of Life and breathe in the aroma of the Tree of Life which blooms and produces a different kind of fruit each month? It will be in a state of perpetual bloom and its fragrance will waft across the glorious city when the soft heavenly breezes blow.

I am told the Rose of Sharon gives its grand, scent only when it is crushed. Jesus, the eternal Rose of Sharon was crushed for our sins and His sweet, ambrosial bouquet will fill every room of our home in the New Jerusalem.

Strange as it may seem, the sense of smell is more acute than any of our other senses for activating the memory process. Odors are more permanently imprinted in the memory section of our brains than what we see, feel, taste or hear.

The smell of certain brands of baby powder will cause you to have a flash-back to the times when your children were small. After a bath you toweled them off and sprinkled their little bodies with powder. Those pleasant memories will make the corners of your mouth curve upward and if you're not careful a smile will dance across your face.

The carnation is one of the least popular of all flowers, not because it isn't hardy and beautiful, rather because people associate its fragrance with funeral homes and the deaths of loved ones.

Heaven, by contrast, will have no unpleasant scents. You've heard the saying everything is coming up roses? Over there that will be true. Every sight, sound and smell will be exhilarating.

Touch—it's a God given sense.

One of the most wonderful gifts God gave to man is the sense of touch. From our eyelids to our earlobes to the smallest toe on our foot we have unbelievable sensory perception. Our body is a magnificent feeling center that responds to heat, cold, fire, wind, rain, soft, hard, wet, dry, sharp, dull and a myriad of other objects and surfaces.

Without the aid of the other senses we know by touch what we are feeling, be it a blade of grass, a petal from a flower, a feather or a hair from a horse's mane. So acute is the sense of touch that we know it even when a small insect is on the tips of our hair.

Can you imagine what it will be like when we move into our celestial bodies, walk down golden streets, listen to angels singing, smell the fragrance of the eternal Rose of Sharon and feel the fabric of the robe we are wearing?

Just thinking about it reminds me of a song we used to sing in the south.

> Heaven is better than this,
> O my, what joy, what bliss;
> Walking on streets of solid gold,
> Living in a land where we'll never grow old;

Heaven is better than this,
Oh my, what joy, what bliss;
I love the saints and the preachers too,
But heaven is better than this.
(Heaven is Better Than This, Joe Moscheo)

Alive—when dead would be better.

Sadly, those who miss heaven will still have their five senses to contend with. Jesus told the story of a man who missed heaven and from hell his conversation showed that he could see, hear, taste and feel. While nothing is said about his sense of smell, if all his other senses were alive reason would have it that he was equally tormented by the smell of fire and brimstone burning the flesh of the doomed. He was alive in a place where it would have been better to be dead than dying eternally.

I have purposely waited to talk to you about the sense of taste until now because it is without a doubt one of the most enjoyable senses God created in us. Think for a moment how unexciting, how grossly unjust life would be if you had no sense of taste. To me this sense is sensational.

You can tell by my size I enjoy eating. I didn't get to be two hundred fifty pounds by routinely missing

218

the dinner bell. I'm not one to gobble down what is set before me. I like to savor the taste of my food.

I won't make your mouth water by talking about thick juicy steaks, sizzling fajitas, shrimp scampi or country fried chicken and gravy, but let me remind you that you are invited to a banquet in heaven.

The Father has planned a marriage supper for His Son and the Church, His glorious bride. Because we are the Church, the marriage supper is for us. If we think we have tasted good things on earth, wait until we get there! We haven't seen, heard, felt, smelled or tasted anything to compare with what He has in store for us when we reach the Golden Shore.

Having been raised in the south, where we get the wonderful Georgia peaches, I can hardly wait to sink my teeth in the fruit from the Tree of Life. For the life of me I can't imagine why Adam chose the Tree of Knowledge of Good and Evil rather than the Tree of Life. You talk about getting short changed. He really got shafted on that deal. When you stop to think about it you realize he was already surrounded by the goodness and mercy of the Lord so the only thing the tree he chose could offer was evil.

Eating from the Tree of Life.

Thank God the Tree of Knowledge of Good and Evil will not be growing in the glorious city but the Tree of Life will line the banks of the River of Life and we will enjoy twelve different kinds of fruit throughout the year.

You may be questioning why I would title a chapter, "The Street of Shame" and then talk about heaven?

I did it to give you a contrast between the two. New Orleans and the New Jerusalem have the same first name but from there the similarities stop. New Jerusalem has no Bourbon Street and New Orleans has no streets of gold. One is filled with righteousness while the other is oozing with raunchiness and filth.

It is difficult to paint a word picture of the glories and the unblemished beauties of heaven and it is equally difficult to paint a word picture of the sin, the depravity, the putrid, perverse, corrupt, violence and rottenness of the French Quarter. If a sin ever existed anywhere in the world, it is alive and well in New Orleans, the city with no boundaries for sin.

The only difference between hell and the French Quarter is, hell is not air-conditioned!

God sent me there with a message for the lost, a love for the sinner, and a loathing for sin. But somehow I bought into the same lie that ruined Adam and began to partake of the forbidden fruit. Not only did I lose my message, I developed a loathing for the sinner and a love for sin.

King Eros

I don't know how to tell you about my only kingship without feeling like a fool and a jester in an ancient royal court. But it's what I was, so here's the story.

Every year New Orleans has what has become known the world over as Mardi Gras. It is a celebration which started in 1857 as a simple parade at the end of the season called Carnival. Today it should be spelled "Carnevil." It is a disgusting spectacle of filth and debauchery to God and every man or woman who has a shred of conscience or an ounce of godliness.

What began as a coming out party for the young socialites has descended to a degree of corruption that defies all human decency. It is enough to make the citizens of the immoral cities of Sodom and Gomorrah blush.

One man is appointed each year as King Eros. He is to lead the parade and preside over the masked ball. Such an appointment would, no doubt, be an honor to some men. But it should have sent up a warning flag telling me I was totally out of step with the Lord.

How could a man of God carry the devil's banner?

First of all, to be approached to participate in such a time of unbridled revelry should have incensed my spirit. It would have, had I been walking in true fellowship with Christ. Where was my mind? What was I thinking? How could a man of God carry a banner through the streets of the city the Lord called him to change, declaring himself an erotic king?

The invitation to be crowned King Eros should have driven me to my knees in humble repentance. It's a miracle that the holy God of heaven didn't strike me dead on the spot when I happily accepted that inglorious title.

I pale today when I remember what a spectacle I made of myself and, worse yet, of the righteous loving Savior whom I was sent to represent. It was as if I shook my finger in the face of God. I was so arrogant, so insolent, so impudent that I thought I could do as I wished and the Lord was helpless to stop me.

Bob Harrington, the man with a vision, the man with a dream, the man with a message red hot from heaven's fiery altar who told the lost of God's love, heaven's beauty, hell's horror, death's certainty and eternity's endlessness, had become one of the devil's prisoners, marching in lock step with those doomed to the dark pit forever.

It is written...

A friend called me recently to read a few lines from a very popular book.

Let me share those lines with you from the page entitled, "Do not be deceived: Bad company corrupts good morals." The author writes,

> We also deceive ourselves when we think we can continually associate with bad company and not be corrupted. When I was a young Christian I used to listen to records by an evangelist in New Orleans who was called 'the Bourbon Street preacher.' This man lived in the red-light district and claimed to have a ministry to prostitutes and other questionable

characters. But according to I Corinthians 15:33, anyone who stays in that environment too long will get into trouble. That's just what happened to this evangelist. He became so entangled with the seedy side of Bourbon Street that he eventually lost his ministry.

The author of the book was almost correct, except I didn't lose out by being among sinners. God called me there and would have kept me unspotted from the world had I sought His face, but I didn't! My demise came when I quit praying, reading the Word and living humbly before the Lord.

My darling mother wept many tears and warned me of arrogance, a warning I failed to heed.

Donned in a white linen suit, I rode a float in the parade and officiated over the masquerade ball. While others wore masks, mine, per the organizer's statute, was a mustache and a goatee. How fitting, I must have looked like the devil's eldest son wearing a white suit rather than the traditional red one.

My heart and spirit should have been dragging lower than the swallow tails of my white linen coat as I rode in that procession. King Eros, synonymous with king of darkness, king of perversion, king of orgies, king of drunkenness, king of homosexuals and lesbians, king of filth, unmitigated filth—and I considered it an honor. What had happened to my once, Christ-honoring soul?

The Street of Shame claims another victim.

It would have come as no surprise had the headlines of the New Orleans newspaper read, "The Street of Shame Claims Another Victim!" The organizers of the parade crowned me "King Eros" but shame crowned me as the "Dunce" of the century. I didn't even notice that I had changed Bourbon Street to the "Street of Shame" and started my long spiral downward toward the gates of hell.

Putting on the dog and eating high on the hog.

If you had asked me, I'd have told you that I was eating high on the hog. The truth is, I was eating from the same slop trough the rest of the devil's crowd eats.

"Frankie" and I had a lot in common. He sang, "I Did it My Way," and I applauded him for telling my story so well in song. Yep, Sinatra and I were like first cousins only as it turned out I was "Not-so-hot-ra."

I was so possessed with money, sex, booze, fame and popularity that I lost everything of value— ministry, family and friends. I was an empty shell, a void, filling space but making no contribution to the world. Shame whittled me down to size and left me a cringing, crying, sobbing failure.

Satan thought he had orchestrated the final curtain call for The Chaplain of Bourbon Street. Suicide raced through my troubled mind like Indy cars on an oval track. To use an old familiar term, I had been ridden hard and put away wet. I was tired of the rat race, tired of telling others how to win but not winning in my own life. I had forsaken the first principle of true success which is:

Godliness with contentment is great gain.

That simple truth had eluded me en route to reaching for the top rung of the ladder to success. I had forgotten that a man can't pull his feet out of the mud by pulling on his own boot straps. I wanted the distinction of being a "self-made man." But what I had made of myself was of no worth to God or man!

Where was God
when I needed Him most?

As the dark clouds of despondency settled around me my doom was certain. Death seemed as close as my next breath and eternity loomed before me as my time on earth came to an end.

So where was God when I needed Him most?

He was orchestrating my return. Rather than try to explain the inner workings of the Holy Spirit, let me remind you of an anthem of the church.

> Great is Thy faithfulness, O God my Father,
> There is no shadow of turning with Thee;
> Thou changest not,
> Thy compassions, they fail not;
> As Thou hast been Thou forever wilt be.
>
> Great is Thy faithfulness!
> Great is Thy faithfulness!
> Morning by morning new mercies I see;
> All I have needed Thy hand hath provided;
> Great is Thy faithfulness, Lord, unto me!
> *(Great Is Thy Faithfulness,*
> *Thomas O. Chrisholm)*

Jesus Christ, in His faithfulness, rescued me, washed me, cleansed me, and turned up the fire in my spirit once again. He helped me move from the Street of Shame to Glory Avenue.

While the Street of Shame, also known as Bourbon Street still exists in the French Quarter of New Orleans and the same sins are committed by multiplied thousands every year, I am no longer bound by them. He drew me to Himself, loved me, forgave me and now I am living proof that any man or woman on the face of the earth can experience for themselves...

"SUCCESS OVER SHAME!"

O Lord, You are forever faithful
to watch over Your Children.
With loving kindness and tender mercies
You direct our lives.

There are times when You seem far away,
almost as if we are forsaken
and alone in a world filled with hostilities
but in Your Word we have the promise
that You will never leave or forsake us.

Help us draw strength from that wonderful truth
and teach others to do the same,
for You are always and forever, the Faithful God!"
Amen.

Chapter Eleven

The Shame of Bad Choices

Early in life we learn to make choices and often to our chagrin we must live with the consequences of the choices we've made.

Some of my earliest memories are the games we played as children. Many of the games at school required team participation which inevitably led to the class "jocks" choosing the team members. I always hated those games because I was never one of the first chosen.

From birth, I was plagued with severe asthma and could not play as hard as some of the other boys. Too much exertion could cause an attack that would send me to bed, sometimes for days. My physical condition created a state of emotional upheaval. I wanted to run, jump, roll in the grass, play tackle football, hit the baseball a mile and run the bases like others but I didn't dare for fear of another attack.

My precious mother was my nurse, often my doctor and always the comforter a boy needs when his world is caving in around him. Unless you have suffered with asthma, you cannot imagine the terror that strikes a child when they can't breathe.

In those days we didn't have the antibiotic atomizers that open up the bronchial tubes. At least, we didn't have them in the little town of Sweet Water, Alabama and if they were available, I'm not sure we could have afforded them. Mom had devised her own method for helping her little boy in times of distress.

Oxygen tent, what's that?

Looking back I marvel at the ingenuity of that lady. We didn't know anything about oxygen tents but Mom made the semblance of one in my room. She would put a high-back kitchen chair on each side of the bed, run a broom or mop handle from one chair top to the other and spread a sheet over them.

By tucking the sheet under the mattress at the foot and along the sides of the bed and under the pillows the tent was secure, then she would put a hot plate and a tea kettle on the chair nearest me. The steam would fill the tent and make it easier for me to breathe.

From time to time Mom would put some Vicks VapoRub in the water. She had a thing for Vicks. She thought if you rubbed enough on the outside, it had to do some good on the inside as well.

I'm not sure but that the rural folks of Alabama kept Vicks in business in those days. It was the number one home remedy for colds, flu, croup and whooping cough. As a rule you didn't find a lot of medicine in the homes of the poor people but everyone had a jar of Vicks.

Mama loved her little Bobby and would sit for hours, gently nursing me back from the devastating asthma attacks. Her tenderness, her concern, her self-sacrificing love, left an indelible mark on my life. She chose to love me and nurse me back to health. A choice I can never forget.

Because of my asthmatic condition I was usually the last boy to be chosen for team play. Nobody wanted me since I was more of a liability to the team than an asset.

Eight scholarship offers

As I grew older we got a handle on the asthma and I became healthy enough to participate in high school sports. My health improved to the extent that I received offers from eight colleges and universities to play football. I wanted to show the boys back home, especially those who never wanted me on their teams, that they made poor choices in not choosing me.

Perhaps that was why I was so elated when God chose me to be on the forefront of His evangelistic team. Me, Bob Harrington, the school jocks last choice was chosen as a first stringer for the Kingdom team.

Consequences, always consequences

For every choice in life, whether good or bad, there is a corresponding consequence. Once I began to outgrow the asthmatic condition and felt good enough to exert myself, I embarked on a journey of making and regretting the choices I made.

The military school in Marion was great when it came to pointing out bad choices and then administering the consequences. Having to suffer, and there is no better word for it than "suffer," for my pranks, taught me to stop mid stream and consider whether a "cute" answer was worth ten or twenty laps around the bull ring.

Oh, that I had learned the lesson well enough to practice it later in life!

I don't mean to leave the impression that all my choices were bad because that's not true. Some were not just good, they were very good.

The night I turned my life over to Christ was the greatest choice or decision I ever made. In a moment of time He took a raw-boned, no-good, hell-bound sinner and changed him into a blood-washed, born-again, Bible-believing Christian. I'm not certain the preacher in the Sweet Water Baptist Church would have welcomed me had he known the full extent of my sins.

This is the amazing part; Jesus knew what a rascal I was and still He loved me. He forgave me and brought me into His family that I might dwell in His house forever.

Another great choice was when I answered the call to preach on Bourbon Street. Even though I became so high and mighty, so arrogant and head strong while

235

I was there, I have no regrets that I said yes to His call.

What would have happened had I stayed humble before the Lord, continued to seek His face and disciplined myself to study the Word daily? The French Quarter in general, and Bourbon Street in particular, would have been impacted tremendously for Christ.

American casualties were staggering.

One of the greatest decisions of my life was to go to Vietnam. The war was taking a heavy toll on American servicemen and women. The daily casualty reports were staggering. Our forces were being wounded, maimed and killed by the thousands.

It was one of the most deplorable times in the illustrious history of this nation.

While our finest men and women, many of whom were just out of high school, were on the battlefield fighting an enemy they did not know in a land most of them had never heard of, the American public was afflicted daily with the treacherous whims of Jane Fonda.

236

Through the years I have tried to be a tolerant man, more especially since the Master has been so gracious to me. But when I think back to what that woman did when our sons and daughters were risking life and limb to defend freedom, it still makes my blood boil. One could truthfully say I was not fond of Fonda.

My friend and pastor, Dr. Grey, tried to persuade me against going. "They have chaplains over there" was his argument. "But they don't have me" was my response. In my spirit I knew I had to go. Someone had to communicate to those brave hearts that everyone back home had not turned against them for answering the call to duty.

The lush green foliage reminded me of home.

Looking out the plane window as we started our descent into Saigon, the lush green foliage reminded me of Louisiana, Mississippi or South East Texas. However, back home you didn't see the plumes of smoke rising from rocket and mortar fire. It may have looked like paradise from the air but on the ground it was a green foliaged hell.

At that time Tan Son Nhut was one of the busiest airports in the world. It was used for military personnel being ferried in and out of the country as well as domestic and international travelers. While the runways could handle jet aircraft, the terminal facilities were a throw back to the black and white movies of the fifties. They certainly were not equipped to accommodate the high volume of traffic.

When the flight attendant opened the door of the plane, it was like stepping into a sauna. I began to sweat profusely.

I know according to etiquette, I'm supposed to say, perspire, but if the individual or group of people who wrote the book on decorum, proprieties, conduct and manners were ever in Vietnam they would know the difference between perspiring and sweating! I started mopping not just dabbing.

When you perspire, you get a little damp under your arms. I was wet all over and that's what I call sweating.

To say I was ill-prepared for what I was getting into is more than a drastic understatement! I was accustomed to the daily onslaughts of the enemy on Bourbon Street but I had never encountered anything like the traumas our men and women faced in that far away, South-East Asian snake pit.

238

In preparation for the trip, letters were written on my behalf to Alabama Governor George Wallace and Congressman Hale Boggs of Louisiana, soliciting their help to get my clearance. Both responded favorably. They too, wanted our fighting forces to know they had not been abandoned by everyone in America for their effort to preserve freedom and democracy in South Vietnam.

Although I contacted Billy Lloyd the Chief Southern Baptist Chaplain in Vietnam telling him I was coming to visit the troops, it was Chaplain Wright, a Lutheran, who escorted me to the front lines and set up the services.

No Baptist bullets or Methodist bombs

When men are dying and bullets are whizzing around your head, the last thing you are concerned with is denominational affiliation. I didn't see one Baptist bullet, Methodist bomb or Assemblies of God grenade. The Vietcong or "Charlie," as they were known, were indiscriminate in who they shot. They wanted to kill every American. And to think, Jane Fonda was out campaigning for them.

Knowing I needed a street-smart guide to help me get around I asked for my cousin Lonny Shoultz. I was relieved when I saw him in the airport. He really looked sharp wearing his Green Beret uniform complete with his side arm. He was an MP as well as a Green Beret.

Lonny took me to his jeep and tossed my baggage in the rear as I climbed into the passenger seat. Trying to make conversation, I said, "Should I fasten my seat belt?"

"No!" He said emphatically, "we can't trust the Charlies. They might flip a bomb or a grenade in here. If they do, you have to get out in a hurry. In fact, if you hear a thump sound inside the jeep, bail out!"

Death was never more than a heartbeat away.

Considering we hadn't seen each other for several years it seemed strange to be talking about survival rather than the family. Death was never more than a heartbeat away, so survival was the main thought in everyone's mind. Until I returned home I didn't realize just how much God was watching out for me.

Lonny gave me a short guided tour of the city before leaving me at the Astor Hotel. The arrangement was that he would pick me up the next morning.

I was deceived by the name of the hotel; I guess I expected something similar to the Astor hotels I had seen in other parts of the world. Believe me that one was a far cry from anything you can imagine.

Rather than being a "five star" establishment it was more like a minus three!

I was relieved to be moving out the next morning, but seedy as the hotel was, it was a thousand times better than where I was going!

In the room I got out of my sweaty clothes, showered, put on the most "civilian" looking threads I had and ventured out on the street. That was not one of my smarter moves.

Buildings, signs—everything looked the same.

I quickly realized I could get lost in the first block especially since every building looked the same. The signs looked like chickens had walked through wet paint and cleaned their feet off on the signboards.

The street in front of the hotel was swarming with cars, jeeps and busses and bicycles. "Gogo-joints" lined both sides of the street and people were everywhere. I looked for a friendly face but the only ones smiling were the pre-teen hookers. Their pimps, usually a "mama-san," had warned them that they had to smile regardless of how bad they were hurting inside.

On Bourbon Street I had seen more than my share of teenaged prostitutes, but to be hustled by mere children made me feel ill. I wasn't ready for what war does to the general populace. Barbarians had turned a peaceful country into living hell.

Because of the war and the struggle for existence men and women were old before their time. They were tired and bent over with the weight of their fears. Life was almost meaningless as they saw their homeland being destroyed day by day. A few minutes on the street that first night gave me a double dose of culture shock.

242

Listening for a southern accent

Back inside the hotel lobby, which I deemed the safest place for me to be, I started looking for a face with U.S.A. written all over it, preferably with a southern accent. It didn't take long to locate one. He was a television newscaster who had broadcast a network hurricane story from his local Texas station and became an overnight news hero. He introduced himself as Dan Rather.

The war stories I was hearing were intriguing but they certainly were not encouraging.

"Up in Khe Sanh, back in '58 the Montangnards lost twelve people to tigers."

"Think that's something? The streams over here have nasal leaches. Get your head under water and you have a terminal nosebleed."

"I hear there's a snake called a Bamboo Viper, they call it the two-step or cigarette snake. It bites you, take two steps and you're dead or it bites you and you've got time to light your last cigarette."

The stories made me wonder what my mouth had gotten me into this time. Had I been given the opportunity to catch the next plane home, I'm not certain but that I would have taken it.

That would have been an eternal mistake!

Morning came very early. Before I finished breakfast and repacked my luggage (I wanted to make sure there were no scorpions hitching a ride among my things), cousin Lonny was knocking at my door. He was there to take me to the airport for the next leg of my journey to the front lines.

No name airline

I thought it rather strange that the plane I boarded was painted with camouflage and didn't have a name anywhere on it. It didn't take too long to find out why. We took off and rather than climbing to a normal altitude we leveled off just above the treetops. We were on our way to Ohn Khe.

Earlier I mentioned the magnificent countryside, but it deserves more than a casual remark. I was stunned with its beauty. No doubt the early explorers saw a land very similar when they came to Louisiana. That was before men turned it into endless plantations.

When I boarded the plane, I had my Bible in one hand and a camera with an automatic flash in the other. As soon as we leveled off, I put the camera to

244

the window to take a series of shots of the lush foliage. With the first flash, the aircraft veered violently as if the pilot was going through an evasive maneuver. Before I could take another picture, one of the crew was hovering over me, "Please don't use the flash, we thought we'd been hit by a missile!"

Now if a statement like that doesn't make you sit up and take notice, your "noticer" is either broken or it's totally out of whack.

At Ohn Khe we landed on a steel mesh strip and I was met by a Lutheran chaplain named Wright. He gave me a brief tour of the area to help get me oriented and explained that I should not walk into the woods.

That all seemed well and good to me until he further explained that there were no toilet facilities. So for privacy, it was necessary to go into the woods. Either no one had thought of digging latrines or else everyone was so busy fighting they had no time.

Front line tent meeting

Chaplain Wright pointed out a large tent. It was made of cargo parachutes stitched together. He explained that would be the meeting place. I estimated it would seat a hundred or so people. The pews were fabricated from salvaged ammunition cases. The pulpit was built from a 105mm artillery shell. These casings, an uncommon building material available in surplus, found use in almost everything.

I was getting a far different view of military chaplains than I had back in my Navy days. These chaplains often jumped with their men, entered front-line fire-fights and ministered to the wounded before the medics could get to them.

This really was the front lines.

The air was constantly churned by chopper blades as helicopters took off and landed and others flew over the area spraying defoliant, creating a buffer zone between the camp and Charlie. This really was the front lines and it was nothing like I could have ever imagined in my wildest dreams. Dreams? Maybe I should say nightmares!

From the woods, I could hear sounds like something was falling into or through the trees. When I inquired, they told me it was limbs falling and spent bullets. Occasionally you would hear the bullets that didn't die in the forest whizzing far too close to your head.

246

My "room" was a small tent with a floor made from cargo skids. It had a little cot. When I say little, I mean petite, tiny, narrow, much too small for a man my size to sleep on. When I tried it, my arms and legs overflowed its capacity and my feet hung off the end.

Then they handed me a side arm and said, "This is primarily for snakes but if you see a human being inside, blast him, he's Viet Cong. If you don't get him, you can bet your buttons he's gonna get you." Now that's what I call a great welcome. Snakes, Charlie, small cot, little tent and no toilet facilities. Strange as it may sound, I actually felt safer in my little tent than I did in the Astor Hotel. Not safe, but "safer." Out here no one was to be in my tent. In the hotel, "Charlie" could have come in as a worker and I wouldn't have known the difference.

The list of horrors grew as I listened to the men tell stories of Vietnam. Asian cobras, elephant grass that was so sharp it would cut your clothes and your flesh to shreds, a snake twenty feet long, fungal and gastrointestinal infections so bad that more of the covert Special Forces and Rangers were hospitalized with it than from combat wounds. To tell you the truth I didn't want to sleep that night, even though I was prayed up and real tight with the Lord.

Catching the next flight home crossed my mind more than once in those first few hours but God gave me the strength to stay. He had a bigger plan than I had imagined.

The "church tent" was overflowing with people that night, over 300 by count. My sermon was one of encouragement, to let them know that they were not forgotten by their friends back home or by the Lord. I explained that the majority of Americans were proud of their servicemen and I had come as a spokesman for the nation.

Some won't come back!

Before the first service, Chaplain Wright spoke to me from his heart, he said, "It's important to give an altar call; they'll be going out in the morning and some won't come back!"

A hundred men came forward to receive Christ that night. It was a time when heaven and earth touched for a brief moment. While we sang praises and choruses, souls were made ready to meet Almighty God. The grim news was given to me the next day; seventeen of those who came forward to receive Christ were killed in action.

When Chaplain Wright picked me up the next morning he said, "I want to talk to you." We got into his jeep and started driving down a dirt road. A short distance from the camp, he pulled off the road and stopped the jeep.

When I looked at him, I knew in my heart something wonderful was about to happen. "People are dying all around me," he said. "I'm afraid I will die out here as well. Will you help me to receive Christ?"

On that dirt road, without a sermon or a song, Chaplain Wright entered into a personal relationship with God's only begotten Son.

I'm that man!

Years later, I told that experience when I was speaking to the servicemen at Ft. Sill. No sooner had I finished telling about the part where we stopped on the road and prayed, than a hand shot up in the crowd and I heard a man say, "I'm that man!" Thank God, the chaplain made it through the war.

I was thrilled at the quick way the Lord saved Chaplain Wright. We were like sitting pigeons in the jeep beside the road. It didn't take Wright long to get right. He didn't spend a lot of time pleading his case; he acknowledged his need and desire for Christ, invited Him into his heart and we got out of there.

Back on the road, he told me we were going to the D.O.A. facility, where they prepare the bodies for their return home.

He explained the missions the troops such as those from the night before experienced. Helicopters carried them to the places where Charlie concentrations were suspected. The helicopter's machine gun would spray the area while the men descended on knotted ropes. That way, the men could get into areas where the helicopters couldn't land. But it left them open to enemy fire as they went down the ropes. They had no protection except the cover fire from the helicopter. Tragically, America lost some of its bravest and brightest men in that manner.

The D.O.A. center

Inside the center, Chaplain Wright introduced me to the man in charge of bagging the bodies. He was older than most of the men in the meeting the night before, and while he didn't have to climb down the ropes in the face of enemy fire, he had one of the most difficult jobs a person could ever be asked to do.

I asked the sergeant how it felt to bag all those bodies. "There are no words to express the pain but

I'm a Christian and I feel like this is my ministry. I pray for each family to be able to cope with their loss."

"It must take a great deal of commitment on your part to stay here day after day sending these boys home to their loved ones," I said.

My own son

"I know the pain they will go through;" he replied, "The third body last Monday was my own son."

When he made that statement I did a flash back to the day when my little baby boy died just after birth. We had planned to name him Robert Grey Harrington. We would have called him Grey after Dr. Grey at the Baptist church in New Orleans. Had he lived, he could have been one of the many who died there and the sergeant could have bagged my son.

Before leaving Vietnam, I visited one of the hospitals. What I saw would make a grown man weep. We walked through the open wards where bed after bed was filled with those injured in the war. I witnessed so many broken mangled bodies of precious young men I felt like I needed a doctor to keep me from being sick.

We came to a man that was trussed down with straps. There were wires and tubes going in all directions from his body. He was in traction for multiple broken bones. The tubes were helping to keep him alive.

"What happened?" I asked. He struggled to get the words out, "I hit a land mine but it looks more like it hit me, doesn't it preacher?"

"How did it happen?" "Five of us were searching for land mines and we found one a little bit too late. The other four weren't quite as lucky, if you can call this lucky, I'm the only one still alive."

My next statement was dumb with a capital "D." "The Lord must have really been with you, for you to survive such a direct hit."

Assembly line death

The young man's face showed anger immediately, "Why the hell wasn't He with my four buddies?" His question left me without an answer. When you're looking at assembly line death, "cutesy" preacher remarks are totally out of place.

I realized that was not the time for pleasing platitudes or sugarcoated statements. Seeing the pain on young men's faces trying to reckon with life after losing an arm or a leg or both was heartrending to me. Tragedy and death are always ugly, but on the battlefield it's even more so.

Earlier I made the statement that I'm not fond of Fonda. While our young men and women were giving life and limb to preserve freedom she was going from rally to rally bad mouthing those same brave hearts.

You can imagine how thrilled I was when I heard that Jane Fonda found Christ as her personal Savior and that she is serving Him. It goes to show that His love knows no boundaries. He loved me when I was unlovable and he forgave me of all my wrongs which I'm certain were more than Jane ever thought about.

Back to Saigon

I spent a few more hours mingling with the Vietnamese people on the streets. It indelibly stamped upon me the memory of a gentle people being trampled beneath the heels of uncaring war lords. I wanted to remember the sights, the sounds and the smells of a nation I would, perhaps, never see again. I was engraving on my mind's eye the place where so many of our precious young men and women died. They should be acclaimed as national martyrs.

Walking down the streets, women and children would reach out to touch me, not for a spiritual surge but because I was twice to three times as big as the Vietnamese men. I must have looked like the white version of the Jolly Green Giant to them.

Everywhere I turned, they were cooking rice which was not too bad but in other pots they cooked whatever meat they could find, and I do mean whatever. Snake, rat, cat, dog, monkey, fish, birds—if it was meat, they cooked it. I could have sworn I smelled YUK cooking in some of those pots.

Home...
with memories etched on my heart.

From my window seat I watched the beauty of the countryside fade in the distance. I was on my way home, back to New Orleans, back to Bourbon Street with a multitude of memories etched on my heart.

Not too many months later America would evacuate our troops and suffer its first defeat since our nation was born.

254

Too many questions remain unanswered.

Why go if we're not going to win? Why put one person on the battlefield if there was ever a doubt that we would wear the victor's crown? Was the war unwinnable? I'll, no doubt, never get answers to these and many more questions, but my heart still asks, "Why?"

Flying home from South Vietnam, I reflected on the days spent there and the things I saw; the fear on the faces of men going into battle, the young man who was angry with God for not sparing the lives of his buddies when they hit a land mine, and the sergeant in the D.O.A. center who bagged his own son. The joy of knowing a hundred new names were written in the Lamb's Book of Life and especially Chaplain Wright finding Christ as His personal Lord. I didn't realize it at the time but I was flying from one battle zone to another. I was about to enter the most horrible time of my life. My mistake was that I underestimated the enemy, just as the American Military Brass did in Vietnam.

Invincible!

Somehow in the maze of life, travel, ministry, publicity and popularity I became proud, pompous, and pathetic. I lost touch with reality and started living in my own make-believe world. In that world I was invincible.

Sin and sensationalism became my daily diet. Money flowed in and I spent it at the same torrid pace until shame shackled me and locked me in its tortuous prison.

Bob Harrington, The Chaplain of Bourbon Street, stood at the crossroads and made the wrong choice. For that choice I suffered the terrible consequences.

I was known across the nation and around the world as "The man with the winning attitude," but I became a loser!

The joy, the peace, the tranquility of my soul was sacrificed on the altar of unbridled pleasure. My transgressions against the Lord, my family, my friends and the ministry made me a prisoner on shame's death row.

From tears to triumph

My smile was as phony as a three-dollar bill and my laughter was as empty as an echo in the Grand Canyon. I could still go through the motions but the fire was gone and life had no meaning. Tears? Oh yes, I had plenty of them but they were nothing more than the summer sun melting the winter slush. Shame had me in its clutches; the handwriting was on the wall; I was finished!

> From home and friends the evil spirit drove
>   him,
> Among the tombs he dwelt in misery;
> He cut himself as demon powers possessed
>   him,
> Then Jesus came and set the captive free.
>
> When Jesus comes, the tempter's power is
>   broken;
> When Jesus comes, the tears are wiped away;
> He takes the gloom and fills the life with
>   glory,
> For all is changed when Jesus comes to stay.
>   *(When Jesus Comes, Oswald Smith)*

Shame had me shackled but Jesus broke the chains and made me free.

Through Christ alone I am daily living with...

"SUCCESS OVER SHAME!"

*Dear God, we have all faced
the consequences of bad choices.
Without Your help we cannot make right decisions.
We need guidance from above
and the strength to obey Your voice.
Help us to walk humbly before You
and keep us unspotted from the world.
In Jesus name. Amen.*

Chapter Twelve

The Profit and Loss of Shame

Sammy Davis, Jr. could have taught a class on the art of human survival. In World War II he was a member of the U.S. Army's first attempt at integrating the services. He was cursed at, severely and savagely beaten, and even painted white by fellow soldiers. His treatment was far worse than being turned down at restaurants or being told to ride in the back of a bus.

Much of his life he knew the pain of being loathed by both blacks and whites. When he became a headline entertainer he was too black for white rednecks and too white for the militant blacks.

That tiny little man educated himself and gave sacrificially of himself to the entertainment industry. He was never too high and mighty to stop and give a helping hand to another actor or actress. But his liberality didn't stop there; he was known to encourage anyone on the crew from cameramen to stagehands and grips. He knew he was anything but handsome so he was especially kind to the make-up artists.

Sammy loved life and wanted nothing more than to be loved by the black community, his family, the industry he served, and the people he entertained. Sadly, he was denied their affection most of the time. Over time, he grew to accept the rejection but never understood why. Neither do I, because he was one of the most likeable men I have ever known.

A call from Italy

When I answered the phone Sammy identified himself. He was calling from his home in Italy. True to his nature, he started immediately to make me laugh. We went at one another with one-liners like two boxers exchanging jabs in the middle of the ring until we were both laughing to the point of tears.

"You sure you're 'The Chaplain of Bourbon Street'?" He asked. "You're too funny to be a chaplain!"

"I'm sure," I answered. "At least I was this morning when I put my pants on. (That was before I became a chameleon and changed colors to be whatever the situation called for.) You sure you're Sammy Davis, Jr.?"

"I am the one and only 'one eyed, black Jew' in the world," he answered.

Even though the conversation had been jovial I detected something in his voice that told me everything was not okay. And since he extended an invitation to visit him in Italy, I caught the next flight.

When I arrived at the place where he was on location for a movie, I was so thankful the Holy Spirit had spoken to my heart. I found a man riddled with guilt; on the verge of suicide. The devil had a death grip on him and he didn't know which way to turn.

Pornographic slime

The room where he met me was as depraved as hell itself. I have never seen anything so pornographic. It would have made Larry Flint, the editor of Hustler, drool on his hand tailored silk suit. (I'll tell you about Larry later.) Sammy didn't have just a few lewd pictures here and there; the entire area was covered with such filth you could almost feel the slime oozing off the ceiling and the walls.

He told me later that our telephone conversation gave him the strength to hold on for a few more days. It was a phone call from Rex Humbard that helped me find my way back to Christ several years later. Thank God for Alexander Graham Bell; there is no telling how many lives have been rescued by that one miracle invention.

Our face to face meeting was far different from the phone call. The God of heaven had sent me on a mission to rescue a man from the clutches of a deadly enemy determined to drag him into the eternal abyss.

We sat down and I explained to him the wonderful plan of salvation. Tears streamed down his face as I told him of the price Jesus paid for his deliverance and of the Lord's great love for him. Then I asked him if he wanted to know Christ as his personal Savior.

I'll never forget his answer; "This is what's been missing all these years, **YES!** I want Jesus Christ to be my Lord, but not for just today; I want Him in my heart as long as I live."

Serving Jesus really is fun!

No one enjoys a good laugh more than I do, but witnessing, first hand, a soul being born again, is the greatest joy of my life. Serving Jesus really is fun.

Sammy told me later, that not since he joined Martin Luther King, Jr. on the freedom marches through the south, had he shed so many tears. But they were not for the same reason. During the march, it was fear that brought on the tears; this time it was true repentance.

He related this story later on one of his television shows and invited me to be his guest. I was also asked to be the emcee at a birthday party given in his honor. Some may doubt that he was genuinely saved, but I don't and when I walk down the streets of gold I fully expect to see Sammy Davis, Jr. coming to meet me.

Was he hustling me or did he really want to know Jesus?

Earlier I mentioned the name Larry Flint, editor of Hustler Magazine—here's the story!

I first became acquainted with Larry when I was preaching at the Cathedral of Tomorrow for Rex Humbard in Akron, Ohio. In those days I would go to the raunchiest joints in town to share the Lord. In Akron there were two or three owned by Larry and his brother. Larry's place was called The Hustler. At that time he was just a small time, sleazy strip joint owner.

Back in those days Larry would take pictures of his strippers and give them to the clients. It wasn't long until he had a steady stream of customers wanting photos. It was obvious to Larry that he had a moneymaking opportunity before him. So he turned the photos into a magazine; called it by the club name and the purveyor of filth was off and running. Hustler Magazine became the leader in the field of hard core pornography.

As the publication gained popularity, Larry came up with an idea to have an interview with one of the leading ministries in the nation. He called the Billy Graham Association and asked for an interview with Dr. Graham. Not wanting to be identified with the Hustler magazine, Mr. Graham's associates referred him to Oral Roberts. Again he was refused and told to contact Rex Humbard. From Rex he received the third rejection, but was told to contact The Chaplain of Bourbon Street.

266

I wanted to reach Hustler readers.

When I received the invitation to be interviewed by Hustler I accepted. During the interview, Larry asked me why I didn't turn his offer down. "Why? Because the people who buy your magazine are the ones I want to reach!"

"One thing I insist on," I told Larry, "I want my answers printed just the way I say them; no editing them to fit your magazine." He agreed and we did an interview that preached the truth for the first time ever in porno print.

Althea, Larry's live-in girl friend, was there asking some of the questions since she was a vital part of the operation as far as the magazine was concerned. I could tell from her reactions that the Word was getting to her. After we finished the interview, she told Larry they needed to get married because the way they were living was sin. He agreed and asked me if I'd perform the ceremony.

It was not easy for them to find a church that would rent their facilities to them because everyone knew that Larry was the king of filth. I brought a new, red leather Bible and presented it to Larry at the close of the ceremony as a wedding gift. It was comical to watch his reaction. He did not want to take that Bible in hand. In the church he asked if I could bring it to the reception. At the reception, he asked me to put it on a table in the house. You would have thought he was avoiding the plague.

He told me later it would have given the reporters a field day to get a picture of him holding a Bob Harrington edition red leather Bible.

Back to the interview

As we talked several times, Larry accused me of being in the ministry just for the money. To him, making money was the most important thing in the world. He couldn't imagine a man giving himself and his talents for anything less. Doing what I did for the sake of souls was as foreign to his way of thinking as publishing a magazine without nude photos. We each had a four letter creed that began with an "L," mine was LOVE—his was LUST.

Althea asked me point blank why I kept saying, "Serving Jesus is fun." To her, religion was something for young kids and old people, certainly not for folks like her and Larry. I told her I'd been on both sides of the fence and it was a lot more fun believing than doubting. Her response was "You pray, I'll play." Sadly, the toys she played with took her down a one-way road that led to destruction. A few years later, Larry found her in the bathtub—dead. The last days of her life were a living hell. Her body was weak and emaciated from drugs and a disease she contracted by using a dirty needle. In despair, she took her own life. She gambled with eternity and lost!

A pink jet

When Larry called me he said "Chaplain, I'll send my jet to get you if you'll come and preach Althea's funeral. I couldn't believe my eyes when the plane arrived, it was pink. I asked Larry, "why that color?" He answered, "pink has made me a fortune, so why not my plane?" If you can't guess what he meant by that statement I won't bother to explain. Like everything else he thought and did, it had a filthy connotation.

The funeral was the most peculiar I've ever preached. Several of Larry's former wives and their children were there. It was as if they were doing their duty to him by attending Althea's departure service.

I know the Lord touched Larry's heart during one of our encounters. He prayed the sinner's prayer and even went so far as to accompany me to a success seminar to publicize the goodness of God.

I was one of the speakers at that seminar along with Paul Harvey. When Paul learned that Larry Flint was there with me, he requested that he be moved up in the program to be as far away from Larry as possible. Mr. Harvey wanted nothing to do with the likes of Larry Flint. He has always been careful to protect his image and the publisher of Hustler would not help his untarnished record. His action that day did not change my opinion of Paul Harvey; he was and is, in my thinking, a gentleman and a scholar. His values cannot be challenged. Paul Harvey is a Christian in every sense of the word.

Not long after Larry prayed the sinner's prayer with me, he became friends with Ruth Stapelton-Carter, President Jimmy Carter's sister. Their friendship lessened his need for me although I believe if Larry had a real crisis in his life; the Chaplain's phone would be ringing again. And I want him to know I'm always here to help him. Next time we meet. He will know there has been a change in me, a change for the good.

Was Larry Flint hustling me or did he really find Christ?

Through the years I've been asked by many if Larry really found the Lord or if it was just another of his patented "hustles." Obviously, I can't answer that question; at the time he prayed, I thought he was sincere. I really believed he was calling on Jesus Christ to be saved.

Part of his waywardness could be attributed to my demise. I was his spiritual role-model and when the devil did his number in my life it could very well have had a negative effect on Larry.

My prayer is that I will have another opportunity to witness to him and that he will see the change Christ has made in me. I am not the same Bob Harrington that Larry knew. My life has been transformed. Oh, there are some things about me that are the same. I still enjoy laughing and I can talk faster than most folks can think. And the passion for souls that he saw in me the first time we met is more intense than it was before. I realize that I have to make up for lost time.

I pray that Larry will say "yes" to the urging of the Holy Spirit. The Word was sown in his heart and that Word has never left him. If he will be honest with himself, he knows his life is empty and void. He had a taste of God's glory and nothing the devil has to offer can compare with that.

Is it too late for Larry Flint, the king of filth, the chief propagator of pornography to change? No! It's not too late for him and his case is certainly not too hard for the power of God.

Is it possible for Christ to love a man like him?

YES! Even though his mind is a cesspool of filth and his mouth is a garbage dump of perversity, Christ loves Larry Flint as much as He loves you and me.

A beating heart means there is hope.

As long as there is life and breath in Larry Flint's mortal body there is hope for his eternal soul. I haven't given up on him, my heart cries out to God on his behalf. I want him to return to the Christ of Calvary.

If I could look in Larry's eyes, I would tell him God has kept him alive even though an assassin's bullet found him and left him crippled. God is not willing for him to perish. But the end will come for Larry and if he has not turned to Christ all will be lost.

The list of actors, actresses, singers, musicians and celebrities could go on and on. In those days, my name was constantly before them. They trusted me and confided in me because they believed I understood their pains and sufferings. They told me their secrets and expected me to give them honest answers. I didn't sugar coat the Gospel or make religious excuses.

Hate sin. Love sinners!

If there was one thing the Lord taught me, it was to hate sin but genuinely love the sinners. Whether on Bourbon Street or Madison Avenue, in strip joints or palatial mansions, the message had to be the same, "Hate sin. Love sinners!"

I wanted to have that uncanny ability of the Lord. While never compromising with sin, He could speak to a harlot and make her feel like a lady. And as long as I gave Him the glory, He used me to touch lives. When I began to accept the praise and glory for the things he did He withdrew His hand and the glory of His presence departed from me.

One of the first lessons an accountant learns is to prepare a P&L or a profit and loss statement. No business can exist without knowing where the profits and losses are coming from and how to control them.

Selling insurance taught me the importance of profit and loss in a hurry and I liked the profit part. It was a simple equation; you had to sell more insurance to stay in the profit margin. If you fooled around, you were on the wrong side of the ledger in a hurry.

There was no reason for me to change directions; God was blessing and souls were being saved. My parish grew from Bourbon Street to every city in the U.S. Cards and letters came from every part of America telling me what was happening in men's and women's lives. Many had given up in despair but the Word of Life touched them and gave them hope again. But bullheaded Bob thought he could make it on his on—and God let him try!

"I will set no wicked thing before my eyes."

Long before Bob Harrington drew his first breath, a wise sage in the Old Testament issued a warning that I should have memorized and reviewed daily.

He said:

> I will set no wicked thing before my eyes: I hate the work of them that turn aside; it shall not cleave to me. *(Psalm 101:3)*

274

How could I read that verse and not take heed? The Word was telling me the eye is the gateway to the soul. Any man or woman who gazes long enough into the pool of sinful pleasure and admires the unrighteousness of the evil one is asking for trouble. Sin is not a coat that you put on and take off at will. It never remains on the outside of the body. Rather, it acts fast to enter the heart and contaminate the soul.

All the years of service to Christ meant nothing to me. All the wonderful things He had done for me personally meant nothing. All the souls He had saved through my ministry meant nothing. I was hell-bent on doing my own thing, my own way.

Sin bankrupt my soul.

Day by day carnality grew stronger and spirituality grew weaker until sin bankrupt my soul.

Down to the depths of darkness,
Down in the pit of shame;
No one to lift from me my load,
No one but me to blame;
I chose to walk the sinful path,
I played the devil's game;

And would have sold my very soul,
For wealth and worldly fame.

Selected

When I penned the title of this chapter, "The Profit and Loss of Shame," I wanted you to see who profits and who loses when shame enters a life. From first hand experience I can assure you the devil is the only one who profits when a man or woman decides to forsake the Lord and do their own thing. The shortest route from the winner's circle to the loser's corner is the path of sin.

I sat in the loser's corner wearing the robe of shame. Sin reduced me to a nobody on the endless road to nowhere. Sin blurred my vision and spoiled my dreams. I was a "has been," a "could have been," a "should have been," until Jesus washed away the stains of sin and pointed me in the right direction again.

Four traumatic experiences

While doing my own thing, I experienced four traumas I would never have had to face had I continued to obey the voice of the Master.

276

1. Emotional torment
2. Physical anguish
3. Relational torment
4. Spiritual torment

With each trauma I became more lost; my world continued to crumble and fall in on me. I found no profit, only loss from the countless deeds of unrighteousness. Death stalked me like a lion stalks its prey. My eyes were hollow, my steps faltered and my heart sank in despair.

The vibrant man known to the world as The Chaplain of Bourbon Street had sold his soul and was no more. I was nothing, a vague memory living in an empty shell until I turned to the Man of the Ages—Jesus Christ. In Him I found life, forgiveness, and renewed peace.

Redeemed!

At last I knew the true meaning of the great anthem of the church written by Fanny J. Crosby.

I think of my blessed Redeemer,
I think of Him all the day long;
I sing, for I cannot be silent;
His love is the theme of my song.

Redeemed, redeemed,
redeemed by the blood of the Lamb.
Redeemed, redeemed,
His child, and forever, I am.

(Redeemed, Fanny J. Crosby)

Jesus Christ purchased me back from the place of waste and has given me the desire to win again for Him.

My message to every man or woman who has taken the wrong road and is suffering the dire consequences of bad choices is: you too can experience...

"SUCCESS OVER SHAME!"

O God, our Father,
Help Your children to see and understand
that there is no profit in shame.

Help them to turn their hearts to You;
wash them in Your precious blood and
rekindle the flame
of the Holy Spirit in their lives.

We have but one life,
so quickly it is past and gone
Help us to live it for Your glory
In Jesus name I pray! Amen.

Chapter Thirteen

The Lowest Point of Shame

Gracious, gentle and good are the three best words to appropriately describe my mother. Throughout her life, even before she was saved, she was a gracious lady, always ready to help those in need.

Mama came from strong German stock. Her father was a six feet six, three hundred and eighty pound man with the brute strength of a team of Missouri mules. Grandpa was the engineer on a steam locomotive. Folks in rural Alabama used to say if his engine ever ran off the tracks, old man Shoultz would just pick it up, put it back on the rails and keep going.

Early in life I developed a strong bond with my mother. Perhaps it was her gentle, loving care when an asthma attack would have me struggling for my next breath. A boy could never ask for a mother to do more. My dad, my brother and I never doubted her love. It was evident in everything she did.

50 cents a day

My earliest recollection of Mom was the way she worked helping Dad through the tough depression times. He worked at the sawmill in Coxheath, Alabama until it shut down. To supplement Papa's meager income during those lean years, Mom worked for the W.P.A. planting trees for fifty cents a day. It was back breaking labor, but she never complained.

If a boy ever had a heavenly relationship with another human being, I did with my mama. She was my hero, my buddy, my teacher and my friend.

Failing her, and that's what I did when I started my wayward journey, was one of the great tragedies of my life. Of all the people in the world I didn't mean to hurt it was her. But that's what sin does. When you and I turn our back on the Lord and walk in the lust of the flesh we become vessels of destruction. We lose sight of others and become callous in our spirits to the point that we don't care who we hurt.

My sin and rebellion brought pain to the heart of Jesus, my blessed Redeemer! It brought pain to my wonderful mother and it brought anguish to my precious children, but I was so blinded by my own desires that I couldn't see the damage I was doing to others. Like a hog running to a trough of slop, I ran to sin. I wanted what I wanted, when I wanted it and didn't care who I hurt in the process. God, mother, wife, children, friends or lost souls; nothing mattered but the satisfying of my twisted, tormented, sin-wracked soul.

Oh, the pain, the hours of turmoil I went through when I realized what I had done.

There were times when it would have been easier to die than to face another moment of my shame and humiliation.

Shame came over me in waves like a tumultuous sea. I was convulsed by my wrong doings.

A lonely island

But where does a man turn when he has rejected God and turned against those who loved him? I became a lonely island in the midst of a storm-tossed ocean. Nothing could save me from the angry waves.

The hurricane of darkness enveloped my soul and the howling winds of adversity blew relentlessly in an effort to destroy my very existence.

Where was the once happy man who loved Jesus Christ more than life itself? Where was the man who lived with fond memories of a mother who had sacrificed so much to make our home a safe haven, a place of comfort?

Where? He had become a fast-talking salesman for the devil. While most folks want to trade up in life, the Chaplain traded down. Down from a faith-filled, Christ-centered life to a sin-seeking, pleasure-crazed, faithless one, devoid of purpose or direction.

Mama was not the emotional type. Her strong German upbringing required her to always be in control of her feelings and never let others know what was going on in her mind. As children, my brother Jerry and I never saw Mom and Dad hug and kiss.

The most I ever saw her cry was when she signed for me to go into the Navy. I remember her weeping hard as if she would never see me again. Mama knew far more about the war than I did and she was keenly aware that I might not ever come home. She was so thankful for my safe return that she and Papa took the train from Alabama to San Diego to meet me when I was discharged.

The shutting down of the Coxheath sawmill was the best thing that could have ever happened to our family. Until then, my dad was content to live like the rest of the folks in rural Alabama—up in the morning, work all day for a paltry sum and "barely get along on barely get enough."

I owe my soul to the company store.

You may remember the song "Sixteen Tons" made famous by Tennessee Ernie Ford. The closing line was, "I owe my soul to the company store."

He was singing about the coal mines, but the same held true for those working in the sawmills. Everybody was paid with script. Script was a kind of "private" money that had to be cashed in the company store.

Between paydays everybody shopped for groceries, clothes or whatever they needed. Notice, I said "needed," not what they wanted, at the company store. When they got paid they would settle up with the store keeper from their script. If there was anything left, which there seldom was, they could think of buying something they wanted.

A true entrepreneur

Papa was a victim of the poverty-encased environment. He had known hard work all his life but for all that hard work he had never been able to put more than two nickels together at a time.

When the sawmill shut down something happened. Papa listened to a voice inside his head or his heart that gave birth to a true entrepreneurial spirit. He saw the chance to break the bondage of poverty and make more than just a living.

In an earlier chapter I told the story of Papa's first venture into business and how it miserably failed. The failure however was not due to his or Mama's carelessness or lack of hard work. It was simply because the poor folks in our part of the country needed more than they had money to pay. The deficit got so big that we had to close the store.

That one failure didn't daunt the spirit of Mama and Daddy. They simply went to another town where folks had a steady income and opened another business.

L. S. General Mercantile Store.

If anyone ever doubted that Daddy loved Mama, all they needed to do is look at the sign he put up: L. S. General Mercantile Store. The L. S. was Mama's maiden name, Ludie Shoultz.

You talk about a general store; we sold everything from slop-jars to turnip greens. It was there that Mama taught me to sell. After school and on Saturdays I was in the store stocking shelves, cleaning the floor or helping folks find what they wanted. I kept wood in the old pot-bellied stove we used to warm the place.

If the weather was pretty, Mama would leave long enough to go to the house and do the wash on an old-fashioned rub board after boiling the clothes in a big black pot with lie soap. Though not as big as her six feet six father, Mama was as tough as nails. She never shied away from work and in the end it paid off for all of us.

Trumpet and violin

Mama loved music and because she played the piano and organ in the local Methodist Church, she was determined that I would learn to play an instrument of some kind. First it was the violin. I don't need to tell you I never had the makings of a concert violinist. I'm not sure if it was my squawking at having to practice while the kids in the neighborhood played, or the squeaking of the strings that convinced her I needed to try something else.

Gabriel's job was never in jeopardy.

The trumpet was next in line and try as I may; Gabriel never had to worry about me replacing him as heaven's number one player. Like Mama, I loved good music but what I got out of the instruments had little resemblance to music and no one ever thought of it as being good. It was a happy day for me when Mama finally conceded that I was better fit for football than the trumpet or violin.

For all her strengths, Mama had one glaring weakness. She was terrified to cross a bridge over a river in an automobile. I don't know that we ever discussed the reason for her fear but I can remember how she would have Daddy stop the car so she could get out and walk across the bridge.

I believe she had the most giving heart of any person I ever knew. In the toughest of times she always found a way to help the needy. Mama was a jewel of a person and she was a joy to be around.

In my blackest hour of sin and depravity, I tried to erase the memory of her walking down the aisle of the little Baptist Church in Sweet Water, Alabama to accept the Lord as her Savior because it pained my troubled soul.

Mama never wavered in her dedication to Christ. From the night when she found Him, she loved Him with all her heart and became a witness of His saving grace. My sinful ways brought great grief to her and Papa for the remainder of their days.

From transformation to transgression

They were eye witnesses of Christ's transforming power in my life. Then in astonishment, they watched the glory fade, the hope disappear and the joy, which had been my strength, dwindle and shrink until it was no more. They saw me go from transgression to transformation to transgression.

I have wished a thousand times that I could re-live those years and undo the pain I inflicted on my precious mother. I know it's impossible so I'm doing the next best thing; I'm making every moment count for the Master. I can't change yesterday. I can't turn back the pages of time and heal her broken heart but

I can lift up the fallen today and strengthen those who are weary with their journey.

Prior to my fateful trek back into the world of decadence I was known as the preacher that never sugar coated sin. I called it the way it was. Sin was sin! Wrong was wrong! Evil was evil, the devil was bad and God was good, so in all honesty I must speak of my life as it really was. I was a wretch. Sin so captivated my thoughts and ruled my heart that there was no place for righteousness. As completely as I served the Lord before my downfall; I served sin, hell and the devil when I turned my back on Christ.

Greed, lust, emptiness

The Bible says that the "love of money is the root of all evil." *(I Timothy 6:10)* At first I was happy with whatever God sent my way. I learned to live by faith and trust the Lord to meet my needs and those of my family.

As my faith increased so did the amount God provided. I was like a child learning to crawl, then walk, then run. Each step opened new vistas of His wondrous grace but somewhere in the midst of my growing and learning I allowed greed to enter into my life.

290

I had needs, perhaps it would be better to say "wants," that were not being filled as quickly as I desired. At that point, I should have stopped, reviewed the way God had always met the true needs and reassessed what was happening in my life. It got to the point that regardless of how much I had or how much I made, it was not enough. I had failed to learn that satisfying greed is like pouring water in a rat hole; you never get it full.

Allowing greed in my life opened the door to lust. I'm embarrassed to think that such a sinister evil could have ever captured my thoughts and actions. Lust is one of the ugliest forms of sin. It reeks with the filth of the devil himself. When lust rules in the heart of a man it reduces women to nothing more than pieces of carnal flesh. Nothing is sacred when lust rules, not the Word, not prayer, not music, the church—nothing!

Most people think that greed and lust pertain only to money and sex and you can be certain these evil forces are evident in those areas but never think that's as far as they go. Greed has its filthy tentacles reaching into every phase of life, especially when it comes to power.

The pool of self-aggrandizement.

I would lie awake at night thinking of ways to become a more powerful motivator. I plunged into the pool of self-aggrandizement. The thought of being able to control other people's lives was intoxicating to my sin-inebriated soul. I wanted power and money. Not just more—I wanted more than more!

When my soul was in tune with the Lord, I could preach hell so hot you could feel the fire, smell the smoke and hear the groans. And I could make heaven so real you could almost see the Pearly Gates, hear the angels singing and tiptoe into the River of Life.

In those days I preached with such passion and anointing it made Jesus so alive, so powerful, you would want to put your trust in Him.

That's when I got a taste of swaying an audience; I could make them laugh and cry and have them ready to shout the house down.

I didn't fully comprehend that it was God playing the heartstrings of men and Bob Harrington was simply the instrument the Lord was using to touch lives and help them turn to Jesus. It was Christ, not me. As long as I yielded myself to Him, gave Him the glory and kept my ego under control, everything went according to the Master's plan. But when I took over the reins and insisted on running my life, everything I touched went sour.

Greed and the lust for power did strange things to me. I changed from a man of prayer and compassion to an arrogant, self-centered braggart. I needed a new touch from the Lord but what I sought after was a more flattering picture of myself. I started playing rather than praying and sinning rather than reproving the sins of men.

The root of all evil

I bought into a popular minister's lie. He said "It's the LACK of money, not the LOVE of money that's the root of all evil!" It sounded cute and even though I knew it was wrong to tamper with or change the Holy Bible, I liked the idea because by then the desire for money had become a driving force in my life.

Money, sex, booze and the quest for power became my short, medium and long range goals. I kidded myself into believing that when I had those things I would be happy and content. The truth is, one woman or a hundred women cannot satisfy the demon of lust any more than a dollar or a billion dollars can slake the thirst of a greedy person.

Appeasing my appetite for sin was like pouring gasoline on a fire. The more I poured, the hotter the fire of lust, sin and greed burned. I tried but I couldn't find the illusive place called satisfaction. I would tell myself that just one more bottle of liquor, one more sexual conquest, one more hundred dollar bill in my pocket and I'd be home free.

Lucifer's laughingstock

The sad truth is I bought into a miserable lie. And I became Lucifer's laughingstock.

On and on it went like a cheap carnival merry-go-round until I was sick and wanted to stop the charade, but by then a different die had been cast. I had made power, money, booze and sex my gods of choice. They ruled my life with an iron fist. Where once I had known love, tenderness and compassion from the God of heaven, those gods beat and battered my soul. I was driven, tormented and troubled. Sleep fled from me like a frightened bird and the voracious appetite I had enjoyed from childhood was nothing more than a distant memory. My desire for food had given way to the craving for sin.

Then shame came with all its pain and the feelings of remorse. I had failed one of the dearest people

God ever let live on the earth—my beloved mother! She drew her last breath knowing that her son, called of God and chosen as a vessel of righteousness, had played the part of a fool. Like Esau of Old Testament fame, who sold his birthright for a bowl of soup, her son traded the precious anointing of the Holy Spirit for a mess of the devil's stew.

I wanted to tell Mama how much I loved her, I wanted to take her in my arms and pray the prayer of faith for her. I wanted to call on the living God to have mercy, but remember I had made a pact with the angry gods of sin and pleasure. The hateful lords of my soul made no provision for the anguish of my heart. They told me my answer was in the next bottle. I was hooked, trapped, bound and being offered on the altar of hell's shameful lies.

I felt deep pain when I heard anyone sing "Suppertime."

> When I was just a boy in days of childhood,
> I used to play till evening shadows come.
> Then winding down an old familiar pathway,
> I heard my mother call at set of sun:
>
> Come home, come home, It's supper time,
> The shadows lengthen fast.
> Come home, come home, It's supper time,
> We're going home at last.

In visions now I see her standing yonder,
And her familiar voice I hear once more.
The banquet table's ready up in heaven,
It's supper time upon the golden shore.

(Suppertime, Ira Stanphill)

Sin gripped me with its powerful claw and held me beneath its dreadful sway until shame filled my mind with the idea that suicide was my only escape.

Lonely, heartsick, tired of the rat race and weary with the toil of my journey, I was ready to cash in the last chips of life and end the terrible saga on the pavement below. Who would know and who would care? No one! I was lost on the sea of sin and no one cared for my soul! That's what the voice of my grueling taskmaster told me.

No one except One.
The One I had rejected!

Even though I had disowned Him, He remained faithful to His promise. He came to me in my darkest hour. He gave me peace and taught me that I could have...

"SUCCESS OVER SHAME!"

Eternal God, Father of Light and Life,
reach out in mercy to that man
or woman whose life is in shambles
because of ungodliness.
Forgive the wrong doings and
wash away the stains of sin
in the precious blood of Your Son, Jesus Christ.
Amen!

Chapter Fourteen

Building Back from Shame

"No man was stronger, no man stood as tall, no man could heal the hurts and drive away my fears like my daddy; he was my Superman!"

"Was! Was, as in past tense! Was, as in another lifetime, in eons gone by, he was my Superman! Until sin entered into his life and robbed me of my most treasured possession. Sin took my daddy away from our home and family, away from the ministry, away from God!"

That was the testimony of Mitzi, my youngest daughter. It was as though I cut out her heart and cast it on the ground without a second thought. Oh no! I didn't mean to hurt Mitzi or her sister Rhonda. I didn't mean to hurt their mother, my wife, Joyce.

It wasn't that I awakened one morning and said, "Today Bob Harrington will break his marriage vows, chase every skirt in town, drink booze until he is loop-legged drunk and sell his soul to the highest bidder."

No, no, no! My slipping back into sin, back into slavery wasn't something that happened suddenly. The devil was not so dumb as to think he could capture me in a moment of time. He had to be clever; he had to be patient and lead me down the slippery path gently or I would have bolted from him and ran quickly to the Father for safety.

Was it a flaw in my character, a weakness that had always been there waiting for just the right moment to manifest itself?

No! When Christ saved me, He did a complete work of regeneration. He didn't save certain parts of my heart and leave darkness in other parts. He saved me from the guttermost to the uttermost! I was as much saved as I will be when I walk the golden streets of heaven.

Consumed with a passion for souls.

In those days my whole being was consumed with the desire to win the lost to the Savior who had miraculously broken the bands of sin off my life and filled me with Himself. I wanted every man, woman and child to be saved. My goal in life was to bankrupt hell and populate heaven! I saw every man, woman and child as a likely candidate to be won for Christ. The devil had a different road for me to travel.

Sin didn't jump off a roof-top on Bourbon Street and land on me; it started when I became so busy that I neglected prayer and Bible study. If someone had said to me, "Bob, you are not spending enough time on your knees!" I would have told him that you're as goofy as a bed bug. If there ever was a man on fire for God it's me.

My problem was that the busier I got the "m" in "me" became capitalized. As that happened, all of the things precious to my heart were relegated to a secondary place. I lost sight of my children, my wife and the ministry God had so generously entrusted to me. Everything of value took a back seat to the demons that were vying for the control of my spirit, my soul and, ultimately, my life.

Did I purposely walk away from God?

A thousand times, no!

I was busy for Him, busy winning the lost, busy for His Kingdom so busy that I lost sight of the true values of His Word. I had so many "important" meetings that I didn't have time to read the Book. My schedule was so packed that there was no time to pray.

Too busy to pray and study.

At first, it was only a day here and a day there. It wasn't that I quit praying and reading my Bible altogether. At first, all I did was put them off until the appointment was over. But before long, the appointments ran together. One day led to another and another and another until a week passed and then a month.

No man can survive the temptations of hell unless he bathes himself in the Word of God on a daily basis and purges his heart through prayer. Anyone who thinks he can stand against the forces of darkness in his own strength is a fool!

Natural man is no match for the fallen angels. The demons of darkness were not impressed by my wit and they were not conquered by the intelligence of this mortal man. Which of us would last a minute in the ring with the prince of devils? Even my six feet six inch granddad would have looked puny beside Lucifer.

So, what made me think I could stand without the whole armor of God? The truth is I quit thinking rationally. I became obsessed with the desire for fame and fortune. If I had a bottle in my pocket and a pretty woman on my arm I was invincible.

The big red "S" on my cape stood for shame not Superman!

To my little girl, I was Superman but, in reality, the big red "S" on my cape stood for "SHAME." It could have stood for STUPID just as easily. I was as dumb as a rock. God gave me a ministry that was destined to shake cities for Christ and I squandered it on the most depraved, wretched lifestyle imaginable.

When Jesus told the story of the prodigal son, the man who wasted his inheritance on wild, unprincipled living, He was also talking about me. I was a prodigal son, but I didn't stop there! I was a prodigal husband and a prodigal father. I took my spiritual inheritance and my children's spiritual inheritance and spent it in a hellish manner.

Clothed in the guilt of my sins, I tried to put the blame on others. I told woman after woman that my wife didn't understand me. I failed to tell them that while I was playing the game of sin, she was at home praying for me and taking care of my children.

I complained that pastors didn't understand the terrible pressure I had of raising the finances for a national ministry. Little did I realize how many of those pastors would have given their eye teeth to stand before a stadium full of people and proclaim the Gospel.

Was it that I was so much better than the least one of them?

No!

It was the unmerited favor of God at work in me! He had especially anointed me to reach the masses. In my prodigal lifestyle I wasted my opportunity to do something great for the Kingdom of Heaven.

Oh, the pain I caused in the life of my youngest daughter with my wayward living. To discover that her Superman really wasn't as super as she had believed him to be! And that his heart of stone was even worse than his feet of clay.

Shame follows
on the heels of sin—always!

When the reality of my sinfulness set in so did shame. Shame for my sin, shame for my callous lack of concern, shame for the trauma, the heartache, the disillusionment I had imported into the lives of my innocent children. I was no longer fit to live. Death would have been a welcome deliverance from the drudgery of living in my shameful condition. I wanted to die! Thank God I didn't because I was not prepared to meet Him in my degenerate state.

How many times I wanted to take my precious Mitzi in my arms and tell her I was sorry for failing her. I longed to look into her beautiful eyes and tell her that I still loved her and that her superman, her hero, would some day make her happy again. But my shame was too great.

My other daughter, Rhonda, had leaned more heavily on her mother throughout the years and, while she mourned the loss of her godly father, she was not as devastated as her younger sister.

By the time I began drifting out on the sea of sin, Rhonda had met and married a young man dedicated to Christ and devoted to her, so she had an anchor to cling to.

The deeper I sank into the quagmire of hell's dungeon the closer she and Chuck drew to each other. They had seen God work in my life and they knew the enemy could and would trip them up if they didn't hold fast to their devotion to Christ's Kingdom.

One of the few bright spots in those lonely years of suffering and shame was to see what the Lord was doing in those two young people. The blessings of Christ were bestowed upon them immeasurably because of their commitment to put Him first in their marriage, to wholly follow Him and to cherish one another. Rhonda has become a gifted author and speaker and Chuck is the president of New Orleans Baptist Theological Seminary.

Rhonda and Chuck embraced everything I walked away from: godliness, peace, contentment, fidelity, trust!

I chose money, drinking, carousing, flirting and filth. They chose righteousness! They woke up daily to face brand new challenges. For me it was a challenge to even wake up. They loved life; I feared life and longed to die.

Like grains of sand slipping through an hourglass, my life was slipping away! All that was left was the empty shell of a man called of God and anointed by the Holy Spirit to reach a lost and dying generation.

Passionate for sinners
or a passion for sin?

The man with a passion for sinners lost his way and became a wretched sinner himself. The Chaplain of Bourbon Street was gone forever! The Bob Harrington of yester-years was no longer there.

Lost, lost, lost on the sea of sin and depravity! Lost from family and friends who really cared. Lost from the safe, loving arms of Jesus—LOST!

No words can express the pain, guilt and shame of a prodigal father living in a pig pen. I know the utter futility that plagued the original prodigal. I too would fain have filled my belly with the husks the swine ate. I was there! I lived with the porkers, wallowed in their mud-hole, feasted on the same slop and drank the same swill.

Sin took me farther than I wanted to go, kept me longer than I wanted to stay and charged me more than I wanted to pay. I came to the devil's dance and had to pay the fiddler!

Where was the Lord?

Where was the Lord when all of this was taking place? Where? He was waiting for me to reach the lowest depths of hell on earth! Waiting for me to look up from the dungeon floor and see His nail-scarred hand stretched out to me. Waiting for me to call on Him to forgive my sins and take me back into the heavenly fold.

Oh yes, I was a prodigal son, a prodigal husband and a prodigal father who squandered his inheritance on sin and wicked pleasure. But to the Great Shepherd I was a sheep, a lamb that had lost his way.

The song writer so aptly wrote:

> Safe were the ninety and nine in the fold,
> Safe, though the night was stormy and cold;
> But said the Shepherd,
> when counting them o'er,
> "One sheep is missing:
> there should be one more!"
>
> The Shepherd went out
> to search for His sheep,
> And all thro' the night on the rocky steep
> He sought till He found him,

> With love-bands He bound him,
> And I was that one lost sheep!
> (That One Lost Sheep,
> L. Phillip Knox and Toral Seat)

If ever a song told the story of a man's life, that one was written about me.

The thing most amazing is that as wicked as I was, the Shepherd never stopped looking for me, the Father never stopped loving me and the Holy Spirit never stopped tugging at my heart. The faster I ran from all that was right and holy, the farther I tried to distance myself from all that was good and godly, and the more my conscience plagued me and made me long for home.

The Lord must have poured a whole bottle of super-glue on a sheet of conviction and stuck it to my brain. Every sin I committed created revulsion in my spirit. When I bellied up to the bar my soul cried out for mercy. Not one day in my rebellion did I find an ounce of joy! Fun—yes but there was absolutely no joy or contentment for my weary soul.

Then came the moment of truth!

Sin's dark night settled around me and the hounds of hell snapped at my heels waiting for the moment they could drag my tattered, defeated soul into the abyss forever. But God was not finished. He could not, would not allow one of His own, one for whom His only begotten Son died, to be condemned forever in the chains of darkness.

Long before sin entered into my heart and took me spiraling downward toward hell's blazing furnace, God prepared a ransom for my soul. The Cross was my place of refuge, my citadel of hope, my anchor in the time of storm. It gave me strength to rise up from the ashes of a burned up life and live again.

From the pit I caught a glimmer of light as it shone on the Cross where He shed His precious blood for me. The fountain opened two thousand years ago on Mount Calvary, that glorious fountain He opened for the sins of all mankind was still flowing to me.

God would not allow the devil to hold one of his children captive forever. He would not turn His face away and let the darkness win over the Light of life. No, no, no! There had to be a reckoning with the enemy. As bad as I was, as sinful as I had become, God had not forgotten the day I confessed Christ as my Savior.

From that day forward the Father considered me His property.

I'm not saying He overlooked my sins, rewrote His book or excused my iniquities, a thousand times no! God hated my sins as much as He hates any sin but He never stopped loving me. The Holy Spirit never stopped wooing my soul and whispering in my ear that there was food, peace and prosperity in the Father's house. He would never let me get so comfortable in the hog pen of sin that I could settle in and be happy.

Give me what is mine!

The prodigal in Bible times (Luke 15:11-32) had to come to himself before he realized what a miserable failure he had made of himself. Before leaving home his favorite phrase was "give me!" "Give me what is mine, give me my inheritance." In essence he was saying to the father, "as far as I'm concerned you are dead. I don't like your rules; I can make it on my own."

When he came to himself, his vocabulary changed. Rather than demanding what he considered his own, he humbly asked his father to "make" him a servant.

While I didn't use those exact terms, my actions said the same thing to God. How many times did I look into the grief stricken eyes of the Savior and tell Him, "I can make it on my own?"

Frank Sinatra sang the song, but I did it, "my way!" The truth is my way wasn't worth a hoot. I was as miserable as a human could possibly be. I became a "self-made man" but I promise you, a self-made Bob Harrington was not a happy sight. God stepped aside and let me do it, "my way." But my way led to lust which gave birth to sin and sin brought forth shame and death!

How could a man whom God had raised up become such a moral failure? How could a true servant of Christ stoop so low and wallow so deep in the hog pen of sin?

I'll tell you how!

One sin at a time!

I learned the hard way that the Father's house is not next door to the pig farm. I didn't step out His front door and sink knee-deep in the mire! It was a journey in time. Just as His house is not visible from the pig sty, the stench of the hogs never reaches His front porch.

The Lord let me stay there until I knew that Porky was not my best buddy and I was tired of eating sin's slop!

Don't ever think that God can't bring you to the place that you'll say, "I've had enough!" We used to say in Alabama, He can make you holler "uncle!"

Here's the great part, the moment I reached up to Christ, I found He was reaching down for me.

Like the other prodigal, when I came to myself I realized how much I lost when I left the Father's house. I lost everything that was near and dear to me and I knew I needed Christ in my life more than anything the devil and his crowd had to offer. I had learned the hard way that money, booze, fame, popularity, fast cars, sex on demand and beautiful women were not the things that made life worth living. At last I could echo the words of Paul, the great apostle long ago:

For me to live is Christ.... *(Philippians 1:21)*

In order to survive in my new surroundings, the Lord had to be the center and the circumference of my being. I needed Him in my thoughts, my dreams and in all my plans.

I remember so vividly the day I packed all my belongings in a single suitcase, caught a bus to New Orleans and checked in at a downtown rescue mission. I was so near broke that I couldn't get a room even in a flop house hotel. Dressed in a suit and tie and carrying a suitcase, I didn't fit the image of a man needing a room and a meal at the rescue mission.

The Chaplain of Bourbon Street

The woman behind the desk said, "Aren't you Bob Harrington, The Chaplain of Bourbon Street?"

"Yes I am," I responded, "but I'm a little short of cash and I need a place to stay until I get back on my feet."

"Wait right there," she said and turned around to use the telephone. I didn't know that she was calling my daughter Rhonda. "Mrs. Kelly, your father is here at the mission; he is asking for a place to stay."

Rhonda said, "I'll be there shortly!" About fifteen minutes later, she walked through the door, put her arms around me and said, "You're coming home with me, Daddy."

314

The next day or so she and Chuck handed me $250.00 and said, "You may need some spending money." It was as if they knew that God had wrought a work in my life and I was not going back to the world again.

Slop bucket repentance

Through the years I have watched one prodigal after another leave the hog pen carrying a slop bucket with them. They do that because they are not really tired of the hogs. They take the bucket of swill to tide them over when the going gets rough. When the demands of the Father get to them, they can take a little swig of slop. They like to reminisce and fantasize about what they had going for them when they lived in Hog Hollow.

Not me!

I want the world to know that I didn't leave a thing in the hog pen that I want back. Sin led me down a slippery path and shame filled me to the point of despair.

The hog pen of sin was exactly that: a pen filled with nasty, filthy hogs, nothing more and certainly nothing less. Sin had me wallowing in the mud with the pigs, gulping down their slop, slurping their swill, and dying a little more each day.

Enough is enough and I had more than enough of the depraved lifestyle! My soul longed for the one thing the devil can never give—peace! Only in Jesus Christ can a man or woman know true peace. In Him alone is the hope of eternal salvation. Apart from Him there is no real life.

When He turned my heart toward home He filled me with a stronger desire for the lost than I ever knew before. I've seen the results of sin. I know the heartache, the pain and the shame sin can bring on a man when he turns his life over to the devil.

I needed a heart transplant.

What I really needed was a heart transplant and that's exactly what God did for me. He took out that old sinful, pleasure-seeking heart of stone and replaced it with one that cries out for mercy for every disobedient son, daughter, husband or wife.

Oh yes, women too! It's not just the men who forsake the ways of God and run headlong into the hog pen of sin.

316

Women and girls are the targets of Satan as well. There is a welcome sign hanging outside of hell's entrance for every prodigal wife and daughter. The deceiver's greatest desire is to condemn everyone possible to his fiery haunts. He wants men, women, boys and girls from every nation to belong to him for eternity.

My daughter Rhonda rescued me from a Rescue Mission and God birthed in me a desire to rescue fallen men and women from the clutches of sin and darkness. My new heart has me pursuing prodigals in the pulpit, the pew and in the public!

There is hope for the hopeless! There is a light that can dispel the darkest night and lead the lost to the safety of His loving arms. No one is such a moral failure that Jesus can't and won't forgive them and welcome them back.

If I thought an individual could become so wicked that God would give up on him, I'd have to hang up my cleats and say the game is over. The raw truth is, regardless of how bad, how wicked, how ruthless, mean, deplorable and obstinate I became, God never gave up on me. He loved me in spite of my selfish pride and sinful heart.

Jesus Christ claimed me as His own child. He paid the price for my total redemption by His death on the cross and He washed away every sin in His precious blood. I never get tired of the words from that grand old hymn.

> Redeemed—how I love to proclaim it!
> Redeemed by the blood of the Lamb;
> Redeemed through His infinite mercy,
> His child, and forever, I am.
> **Redeemed!**
> *(Redeemed, Fanny J. Crosby)*

Two college degrees

I graduated from the College of Chastisement with majors in Pruning and Purging. I promise you, it's no fun and the tuition is high! But when the Father finishes His masterful clipping and cleansing, the vessel is really ready for service.

He prunes the vines carefully and completely so that when the final twig is snipped away it is ready to bear fruit again.

God never prunes or purges to wound and destroy us, but to make us more fruitful. Sin and its sensations had so twisted my life that He had to cut me down to size and start the process of blessing all over again.

Shame engulfed my soul and held me captive until the Lord liberated me from its suffocating grip. Sin wrote Ichabod (the glory has departed) over the door of my heart but grace, God's wonderful grace, found and pardoned me from all my sin and His blood washed me clean again.

Unconditional love

I didn't know the bitter tears Rhonda and Mitzi shed for me or the terrible ache they felt in their hearts for the hero who had forsaken them and the God he taught them to trust. I had no way of knowing the wondrous work He was doing in my darling daughters during my rebellion. He prepared them to accept me back with the same unconditional love that He had for me.

Friends, family, pastors, fellow soldiers turned away and wrote me off as a lost cause but not God. In the darkest hours of my sinful state He gave Rhonda a divine promise that I would return to Him, to her and to the ministry.

Sin took me down the slippery road so close to hell that I could feel the fire, smell the smoke and hear the cries of the damned, but the devil couldn't drag me through the doors into his blazing inferno. A nail-pierced hand blocked the way! It caught me at the very entrance of the eternal abyss and pulled me back to safety at the foot of the cross.

Tears? Oh yes, tears flowed down my cheeks in torrents. I wept for days over my sinful past and the pain I had caused the heart of my blessed Redeemer but it took more than sorrowful tears.

It was time for the three big "R's!"

REPENT! RENOUNCE! RETURN!

I repented of all my sins, renounced my allegiance to the devil and returned to my Father, my faith and my family.

The blood of Jesus Christ washed me so clean. God's power wrought such a work in my life that I have never desired another sip of the devil's swill. When I returned, I was not carrying the slop bucket from the hog pen. I am free—totally and completely free!

Overcoming the lust of the flesh was the first step in my journey back from oblivion. The next major encounter for my soul was to win the victory over shame.

There are no words to adequately express what shame can do to a man or woman. When I became cognizant of the irreparable damage I had done to the Kingdom of God, and the anguish I had inflicted on my precious daughters with my sin and foolish rebellion, the grief in my heart was more than I could bear. More than once, I wanted to crawl off in a corner and die.

Shame became
my constant companion!

Day and night shame became my constant companion. Shame ate from my plate and laid its ugly head on my pillow each night until the Lord in His infinite mercy brought deliverance to me from the power of shame.

He taught me that the same mercy and grace He bestowed on me to take away my sins would also free me from guilt and shame.

His love made the difference and gave me...

"SUCCESS OVER SHAME!"

Marvelous loving God,
thank You for loving us
when we were lost and unlovely.
Thank You for caring enough
to send Your Son, Jesus Christ,
to die for our sins;
it is not by our goodness
but by Your mercy and grace alone
that we have eternal life.
Amen.

Chapter Fifteen

When Shame
Gives Way to Victory

Disgrace, embarrassment, humiliation...call it what you will, shame by any other name smells the same! It stuck to me like a blood-sucking leech, draining the life out of me, trying to drag me downward to the bottomless pit.

Because of my sinful past, I didn't know of one church that wanted me to darken their doors to even pray. In most of them I was about as popular as a skunk in a hen house. It was as if what I was would rub off on the members. I can't say I blame them for feeling the way they did. I had broken every promise I made to God and men.

My ministry was over, my family was gone, I traded my dreams for a bottle of booze and my name was ruined. If it had not been for the grace of God, the devil would have destroyed my soul in hell.

Not once, but a thousand times, he laughed with glee at my calamity because he knew that by my own strength I could not in a trial of a thousand years, break the stranglehold he had on my life. I was hopelessly bound by the lust of the flesh and the foolish desires of an unrepentant heart.

Only those who have strayed from the Lord and walked the path of disobedience, know how the enemy torments the mind and tries to make you believe that God no longer loves you and that you are lost forever.

Sin, wretched sin

My chaotic, sin-filled style of living made me an easy target for the devil. Once you start drinking from his cup and become addicted to his brew, he will beat on you and inflict more suffering than you can imagine. Had I never known the Lord and His glorious peace the devil wouldn't have tormented me so mercilessly. It was as if he wanted to take out all his vengeance on my poor tattered soul. Thank God for His wonderful love. He wouldn't allow the enemy to completely destroy me. He came to me and with His strong arm rescued me from destruction.

At my lowest point of despair Jesus reached down to me with His nail-scarred hand. He lifted me from the horrible pit of sin, washed the filth from my soul and pointed me toward home. The moment He touched me the miracle started and it hasn't stopped. I am alive today through His abundant grace. The person who thinks that God no longer works miracles needs only to look at the difference He made in my life.

I was sad, lonely, more dead than alive, no one to turn to and no place to go! I was at the bottom of the pit! God knew I would get there. So when I arrived He was waiting for me with so much compassion it broke my stubborn heart. When He poured in His oil of joy, peace flooded my tattered soul and I was on my way to victory over shame.

I wish I could tell you that all my shame was taken away in one fell-swoop but it didn't happen that way. My sins, yes, the blood of Jesus cleansed me from within so thoroughly that not one sin remained to stain my soul. Shame, however, had to be overcome daily.

Remembering the way I had deserted the Lord and my family caused me such pain I could hardly go on living and it was all related to my shame. When I thought of the souls, the precious souls, I had betrayed waves of nausea swept over me, and my shame made me wish I could go away never to be seen again.

The absence of sin
destroys the power of shame.

The devil tried to use the power of shame to lure me back into sin, but he loses his control over men and women when our walk with Christ is honest and from the heart. The moment I fully rededicated my life to the Lord the bands of shame began to be broken. At last I was on my road to complete recovery and total victory over shame.

My redemption from sin and shame didn't mean that pastors opened their pulpits to me or in some cases even forgave me of what I had done. Some considered me a renegade, a turncoat, a rebel and a charlatan and, the truth is, prior to Jesus delivering me when I was at the lowest point of depravity, I was all of those things. I was a rebel! I was a renegade and a charlatan. But the moment He touched me my heart was set aflame and I became a Certified Soul Winner again!

In a moment of time, I was delivered from the desire for fame and fortune, the wandering eye, the pompous attitude, and, most importantly, the "self-will" that spelled my doom. Christ took away all the things that captured my soul and made it wretched in His sight and He replaced those unholy attributes with a passionate desire for Him and true holiness.

I'm not sure I will ever be able to relate to others how close I was to destruction. Let me describe it this way, I had one foot in my personal hell and the other was on a banana peel. Death was lurking at every corner. I was playing Russian roulette with a pistol that had a bullet in every chamber. Sin had so decimated me that nothing was left but the skeleton of a man. I had absolutely nothing worthwhile to live for.

But then, what does a man have to live for when he rejects God, forsakes his family and plays the part of a fool?

Sin deprives. Grace revives!

Sin was a terrible taskmaster. It deprived me of the simple satisfactions of life. One of the great pleasures from early childhood was sitting down to a sumptuous meal but sin changed all of that, I no longer enjoyed eating. I was once a handsome, well-dressed man, but sin wrinkled my face and my dapper attire became sloppy. Mark it down—**Sin deprives!**

327

Thank God! That's not the end of the story! While I cannot overemphasize the truth contained in the statement "**sin deprives**," neither can I overstate the wonderful truth that "**grace revives!**"

While the enemy of my soul and his sneering, snickering imps would have had me cascading down slippery slopes into chaos and utter confusion, God had a different plan. He had a revival planned for The Chaplain of Bourbon Street. The Father never changed His mind about me. Gazing through the telescope of time, the Savior saw the scarred, tattered and burned-out soul of Bob Harrington rise up from the ashes of destruction like the legendary phoenix. God revived my soul and allowed me to begin life anew.

The words of this song so aptly describe my jubilation to the Lord for His mighty acts of love toward me.

> Amazing grace will always be my song of
>   praise,
> For it was grace that brought my liberty.
> I can not know just why He came to love me
>   so;
> He looked beyond my faults and saw my
>   needs.

I shall forever lift mine eyes to Calvary
To view the cross where Jesus died for me.
How marvelous that grace that caught my
    falling soul;
He looked beyond my faults and saw my
    needs.
(He Looked Beyond My Faults, Dottie Rambo)

Read those words one more time, "He looked beyond my fault and saw my need!" My sins had separated me from close intimate fellowship with Him but not from His everlasting love.

Defeating shame is like eating an elephant one bite at a time!

Moment by moment, day by day and step by step the Lord delivered me from the horrible clutches of shame. As I said earlier when my sin was removed, the devil had no power over my life, his stranglehold was broken so he could no longer fill me with nauseating shame. I began to live again!

As His life flowed into me, since "I" was not the most important letter in the alphabet, and fame and fortune were not the driving force behind my actions, His life flowed out of me. Basking in the Son-light rather than a pathetic ten watt bulb of self-importance, my phone began ringing. Pastors called and doors opened for me to minister His love around the country.

At first, it looked as if only the small churches would take a chance on having me but that wasn't it at all. The Lord was showing me that I should be thankful for any open door and that I shouldn't ever feel so important that I would turn down an invitation because a church was small.

With a grateful heart I went wherever He sent me and soon enough three of the nation's greatest ministries called for me to come and minister. I will forever be thankful to Jerry Falwell for having me come to Thomas Road Baptist Church; James Robison for having me as his guest on his national television program; and John Hagee for opening his pulpit at the great Cornerstone Church in San Antonio. It took a tremendous amount of intestinal fortitude for these men to open their doors for me after the life I had lived.

The Lord knew how much I needed to have someone with strong influence to have faith in me to believe that I had really repented and God had changed me from the inside out. Those three men stepped out in raw faith and said to the Christian community that they practice what the Word teaches—restore the fallen brother.

330

Something was missing.

Having traveled the road of sin and degradation, I was keenly aware of the pitfalls along the way. So I carefully avoided any social contact. I wasn't about to give the enemy any occasion to flood my life with guilt and shame again. I went to church, preached, prayed with sinners, and kept my distance from any semblance of wrong.

One night while kneeling in prayer, I opened my heart to the Lord and told Him how lonely I felt inside. It wasn't lust or the wild passions of a soul bound in sin. I was lonely for a companion, a soul-mate, a partner who would share my dream, my vision and my desire to win the lost. Someone who would be a completer not a competer!

This is what is so great about God. He didn't get His feelings hurt by what I said to Him about being lonely. It wasn't as if I was telling Him that His divine presence was not enough to satisfy my loneliness. After all, it was God who said:

> It is not good [sufficient, satisfactory] that the man should be alone; I will make him a helper meet (suitable, adapted, complementary) for him. *(Genesis 2:18 AMP)*

Wow man!

The Bible doesn't give us a detailed report of Adam's first reaction when he awakened from his, God-induced-sleep, to find Eve in the Garden of Eden. All we can do is surmise what he did. One preacher said when Adam saw Eve, he said, "Wow man!" And from his exclamation we got the word, "woman."

One night a friend whom I had known for more than thirty years came to hear me preach in Branson, Missouri. After the service, as I stood at the book stand, she told me how the message had touched her heart and that she had never lost faith that I would return to the Lord and that He would use me again. Then she whispered something in my ear that left me astounded.

She said, "I have loved you for all these years!" I want you to know that her words made me take another look at celibacy. I was preoccupied with winning the lost—that was my sole purpose in life after the Lord delivered me from the slime pit of sin, but her words struck a cord in my soul.

Until that moment, I didn't realize that God had looked on the loneliness of my heart and was sending me a true soul mate, someone who would stand beside me and help me reach out to a sin-crazed world with the message of life.

332

The same powerful God that stretched forth His hand and rescued me from the path of self-destruction sent this lovely lady to be my wife; my one and only sweetheart for the rest of my days on this earth.

There are no words to express the joy that filled my heart when we stood in the great entryway of the Grand Palace Hotel in Branson several months later. My friend, Cecil Todd, of Revival Fires Ministry, presided over the ceremony for Becky and me. As we repeated our marriage vows, I think I was the happiest man on earth. It was during the Christmas season but the lights on the trees were pale in comparison to the brightness of Becky's eyes.

How good and gracious the Lord was to me to bring me a lady of such honor and integrity. Becky didn't see me as a person to compete with, rather, as someone to love, cherish and devote her life to in the service of the Lord.

Look out devil, the CSW is doubling up!

I have read the sayings of Solomon many times but the truth of his words really came to life after Becky and I were joined together in holy matrimony. Let me share some of them with you:

Two are better than one because they have a good return for their labor. For if either of them falls, the one will lift up his companion. But woe to the one who falls when there is not another to lift him up. Furthermore, if two lie down together they keep warm, but how can one be warm alone? And if one can overpower him who is alone, two can resist him.... *(Ecclesiastes 4:9-12 NAS)*

For all those years I thought I could handle everything by myself, but I've discovered that Becky and I are far more effective as a team than I was alone. When the devil attacks Becky or me, he has to contend with both of us; he can no longer single us out. We are a combined force against him and his demons of darkness. When he fills my mind with negative thoughts and gets me to thinking I'm failing the Lord, I have my prayer partner, Becky, to help me battle through his lies.

Take note—any man who wants to be an island unto himself must understand he is a very small piece of real estate!

The thing I failed to realize was that being a loner made me vulnerable to any whim of old slewfoot.

I was the proverbial island to myself. But being an island made me subject to every howling storm. As I look back on my pomposity it is easy to comprehend why I was under water most of the time. I was a small dot on the vast sea of humanity and the tiniest wave swept over my head.

I had to be delivered from me before God could accomplish anything good in my life! My foolish ego had so skewed my thinking that nothing less than the miracle of His grace could change my heart. I needed that marvelous miracle for Him to work through me. In my case the word "**ego**" was an acronym that meant, "**edging God out**!"

With my soul-mate, Becky, beside me I have been able to throw off the last remaining rags of shame. I see life through a different set of eyes and, while I'm not the man I should be and I'm not the man I'm going to be, thank God, I'm not the man I used to be!

Together, we are more than conquerors.

Life has taken on a whole new meaning since the Lord brought Becky to me. I have a prayer partner, a person who loves me and the ministry. My soul is at peace with God and my mind is at ease with my precious wife. We are a team, we battle the forces of darkness together. With our combined faith we are more than conquerors in Christ!

Shame reduced me to a pawn for the devil to use and abuse but God, through His abundant mercy and grace, has caused me to rise above the shadows of defeat and to stand tall for Jesus again.

I was wrong! I acted wrong! I did the things that God despised and I did them with utter impudence toward Him! It was as if I controlled the world around me. The truth is, I had yielded my will to the devil, and he was using his weapons of destruction to wreck and ruin as many lives as he possibly could through me. It's hard to imagine, the man who had once boldly proclaimed the unsearchable riches of Christ, blindly following his arch enemy into the dark caverns of sin and wickedness. But I did and it left me empty inside!

Nothing can fill the God vacuum except God!

Man was created with a "God vacuum" inside his bosom and nothing can fill it but the Lord. From the beginning of time man has tried to find peace and contentment through riches, political power, sexual

336

exploitations, fame, drugs, drinking and a host of other things only to find that the more he does and the more he possesses, the emptier he becomes. This is because nothing can fill the space He created in us for Himself—except God.

Man never finds lasting peace or true happiness apart from the Lord. No amount of wealth, fame, public adulation, power or carnal pleasure can produce inner satisfaction. I learned the hard way that nothing less than Jesus can slake the thirst for eternal life. Nothing less than His divine presence can make the heart happy and free.

Solomon, the wisest man in the Old Testament, set his heart to find the answer to happiness. He married three hundred wives and had seven hundred concubines to try to appease his raging appetite for sex. He declared his pursuit "vanity and vexation." He had such vast wealth that gold was like rocks and silver was as dust, but it, too, was considered "vanity and vexation." He wrote books, sought after knowledge and filled his mind with wisdom beyond anyone of his time and for generations to come. But in the end, he declared it all, "vanity and vexation."

Why did Solomon's quest for fame and fortune, wisdom and knowledge end in such ignominy? Because he left God out of the equation! With all his wisdom, wealth and absolute power as the greatest king of his time, when he forsook the Lord, his wisdom turned to folly and his kingdom crumbled from within.

While I was not a modern day Solomon I, too, forsook the way of the Lord to follow fame, fortune, the pride of life and the lust of the flesh and reaped the same miserable results. I should have learned from his example but I was blinded by my own foolish desires. I was left to wallow in the depths of shame.

Total victory came in three definite stages.

There were three definite stages to my complete victory over shame. The first was accepting forgiveness from God.

I had stooped so low in immorality and wickedness that it was difficult for me to believe that Christ could and would forgive me. My first thought was that I needed to do some sort of penance. Surely as guilty as I had been, as many sins as I had committed, He would require something more of me than repentance. My rebellion had so warped my thinking that I could not imagine the depth of His great love for me. Somewhere along the line I had lost the reality of how great He is. Not was, and not will be, but how great and magnanimous He is!

When you consider where I was and what I had become, you understand the utter folly of my trying to offer anything to Him for the mercy He extended to me. What could I offer Him? I was clothed in the rags of my sin, lost, and lonely within when He reached through time and eternity to rescue my soul. The truth is, had I been as rich as Solomon I could not have paid for my forgiveness. Nothing less than the death of Jesus Christ on Calvary's cross could pay the full price for my redemption.

Forgiving others was easy. Forgiving myself was a different story altogether!

The second stage of victory over shame came when I forgave myself.

This was one of the hardest battles I have ever fought. I had no problem forgiving others but I knew what I had done. I was well aware of how wretched I had been, and the terrible pain and suffering I had inflicted on my children, the Church and my precious Savior.

How could I ever forgive myself? I had seen the hurt in my daughter Mitzi's eyes. I had witnessed the anguish of Rhonda's heart and in the depth of my soul,

I knew I had betrayed hundreds of weak Christians in churches all across the land. To forgive myself seemed impossible I wanted to continue to punish myself for my sins.

Christ washed away all my sins and completely forgave me, but I could not be totally free from the crushing weight of shame until I was willing to forgive myself. He showed me that I had no right to hold on to my shame when His blood had cleansed me. Even though it was the most difficult thing I had ever done, the moment I forgave myself and ceased to carry the guilt, my prayer life changed from doom and gloom to joy and peace.

Restoration—
a gift from above.

The third and final stage of victory over shame came when I allowed His full restoration.

Let me explain!

Even after I knew I was forgiven, there was a nagging fear that I would never be restored to a place of service. Why did the fear of God's rejection trouble me so? Remember, I had been a modern day Judas. I had betrayed the Lord, sold myself to work the works of the devil and run with the hounds of Hades. The sad part is that I knew I was walking in defiance to the Lord! I fought with my own conscience and against the convicting power of the Holy Spirit because I wanted to do my own thing, my own way.

After all that I had done against the Lord, it was no wonder that I had the nagging fear that God would not allow me to return to a place of dignity and service to Him. The question was always before me, "why would He trust a turncoat like me when I had so miserably failed Him and separated myself from Him?"

The Holy Spirit gently revealed God's majestic plan and led me back into the place of His abundant blessings. I will never forget the day the thought occurred to me, "if a man loses his way, what does the Word tell you to do?" Without a moment's hesitation the answer flashed through my mind, according to the Bible we are to restore such a one in the fear of the Lord! Then He asked me, "Does God expect more of you than He will do?"

That question was the catalyst for my deliverance; God would not require more of me than He was willing to do. If He expected me to restore a fallen brother, He would do it for me.

I remember seeing a beautiful baby grand piano in the home of a friend and the fascinating story behind it.

My friend found the piano in an old warehouse where it had been stored for years. It had been brought to the warehouse from a bar. It was in sad condition. The lid had burn marks where cigarettes were carelessly laid and allowed to burn and mar the once flawless finish. Drinks were spilled and no one cared enough to wipe them up-leaving ugly marks. On one side there was a monstrous gash undoubtedly the result of a fight between two drunks. The piano stood silent in the warehouse. Its strings were broken or out of tune; its beauty scarred and gone.

When my friend saw the tired old piano, something stirred within her heart. She said to the owner of the warehouse, "I want to buy it!" The man looked at her as if she had lost her mind. He, no doubt, thought she was a nutcase. Why else would she spend even a few dollars for a worn out, piece of junk from a beer joint? What the warehouseman didn't see was the hidden beauty beneath the ugly facade. He didn't hear the music that still resonated in the sound-board. He didn't know that this abused instrument could live again and occupy a place of honor in a warm, loving home.

The master craftsman

The piano's first stop was the shop of a master craftsman. He carefully sanded away the burns, removed the stains and restored the finish. He replaced the missing ivory and the broken strings and tuned it. When he brought it to her home she sat down and played an anthem of the church.

That which had been used, abused and abandoned to the ash heap was restored! To see it today you would never, in a million years, imagine that it was once a neglected beer parlor music piece.

I was like that beat up, worn out, abused, scarred and abandoned piano. Jesus Christ found me and restored me to a place of divine service for Him.

Grace—nothing compares with it.

I can think of no better way to finish this book than with the words of a beautiful old hymn!

Grace, grace, God's grace,
Grace that will pardon and cleanse within;

Grace, grace, God's grace,
Grace that is greater than all my sin!

(Grace Greater than Our Sin,
Julia H. Johnston)

Regardless of what you have done or how far you have fallen into sin, there is hope for you! The Christ of Calvary is reaching out to you today. Let Him wash you in His precious blood and give you everlasting peace.

By trusting Him you can know...

"SUCCESS OVER SHAME!"

Eternal Father,
May Your mercy and grace flow
from the Cross of Calvary
to Your children today.

Hear their cry and send deliverance,
for these are Your children.

Surround them with Your love
and keep them as the apple of Your eye.

In the glorious name of Jesus Christ I pray!
Amen.